P9-CDV-631

CHRYSLER PT CRUISER

MATT DeLORENZO AND JOHN LAMM

MBI Publishing Company

First published in 2000 by MBI Publishing Company,
729 Prospect Avenue, PO Box 1, Osceola, WI
54020-0001 USA

© John Lamm, 2000

All rights reserved. With the exception of quoting brief passages
for the purposes of review, no part of this publication may be
reproduced without prior written permission from the Publisher.

The information in this book is true and complete to the best of
our knowledge. All recommendations are made without any
guarantee on the part of the author or Publisher, who also
disclaim any liability incurred in connection with the use of this
data or specific details.

We recognize that some words, model names and designations,
for example, mentioned herein are the property of the trademark
holder. We use them for identification purposes only. This is not
an official publication.

MBI Publishing Company books are also available at discounts
in bulk quantity for industrial or sales-promotional use. For
details write to Special Sales Manager at Motorbooks
International Wholesalers & Distributors, 729 Prospect Avenue,
PO Box 1, Osceola, WI 54020-0001 USA.

Library of Congress Cataloging-in-Publication Data

DeLorenzo, Matt.
   Chrysler PT Cruiser / Matt DeLorenzo and John Lamm.
        p. cm.—(ColorTech)
   Includes index.

ISBN 0-7603-0988-4 (pbk. : alk. paper)
   1. PT Cruiser automobile. I. Lamm, John. II. Title.
   III. MBI Publishing Company ColorTech.
TL215.P8 D45   2000
629.222'2—dc21   00-059438

On the front cover: The Chrysler PT Cruiser's styling
defies categorization . . . is it a compact or a minivan or an
SUV? However it's classified, its unique packaging and
styling have made it an instant hit with buyers. *John Lamm*

On the title page: Chrysler stylists gave the PT a
pronounced forward rake, then tilted the rear lift gate
forward to remove the boxiness from the car's shape.
John Lamm

On the frontispiece: The PT Cruiser's grille and muscular
fender bulges add a hint of hot rod styling to an otherwise
tall, narrow vehicle. The result is a distinctive, fun shape
like nothing else on the road. *John Lamm*

On the back cover: The PT's chrome accents stand out
against the bright red paint, lending a classy, detailed look
to a relatively inexpensive car. Body jewelry includes
chrome door handles, the lift gate badge/latch, wheels,
emblems, and the winged badge at the top of the grille.
John Lamm

Edited by Steve Hendrickson
Designed by Katie Sonmor

Printed in China

CONTENTS

ACKNOWLEDGMENTS

This inside look at the development of the PT Cruiser is a true collaborative effort. In addition to taking most of the photographs, many of the interviews with the principals were conducted by John Lamm.

We could not have done this without the help of the many people who work at DaimlerChrysler's Auburn Hills headquarters, chief among them Tom Gale, Executive Vice President of Product Design and Development. In addition to the many PT Cruiser team members who gave generously of their time, special thanks goes to designer Bryan Nesbitt, who gathered up many of the development sketches. We also offer our sincere gratitude to public relations vice president Steve Rossi and his staff, including Kathryn Blackwell and Sam Locricchio, who enabled our access to team members, reams of specifications, and the PT Cruisers themselves.

We'd also like to thank Thos L. Bryant, editor-in-chief of our mother ship, *Road & Track*.

Last, but not least, we'd like to thank our families—Jane DeLorenzo, for providing her copy editing skills, and our children, Stephen and Amy, as well as John's wife, Scheri, and daughter Holly, for their support and assistance.

INTRODUCTION

"WHAT IS IT?"

The question is invariably asked whenever a Chrysler PT Cruiser is spotted for the first time.

It is a small, five-door, front-drive hatchback that grew out of the Neon four-door subcompact program, but which shares very few parts with the entry-level sedan.

It has styling that's part retro, part modern, and part funky. While offering all the space of Europe's hot-selling, one-box minivans such as the Renault Megane Scenic, it has a look that is distinctly American.

It has a place for all your stuff. With flexible seating and a unique five-position parcel shelf, it can haul people, things, or any combination of the two.

It represents a new way of thinking about small vehicle proportion because it's tall, providing ease of entry and exit and above all, an upright seating position that offers a commanding view of the road.

It functions as a minivan, but looks like a retro-styled truck. In fact, the government classifies it as a car

and a truck. The truck certification by the National Highway Traffic Safety Administration allows the company to sell more V-10 Rams and still meet fuel economy standards. And yet the Environmental Protection Agency considers the PT Cruiser a car. Consequently, it meets all car clean-air and safety standards.

It was developed as part of a secret four-year project, however pieces of the project were dangled beneath the public's nose all along. Former Daimler-Chrysler Chairman Bob Eaton likes to say, "It was developed in plain sight."

In fact, the first public showing of the concept came in January 1997 under the guise of the Plymouth Pronto—a tall five-door hatch developed off the Neon platform. In March 1998, Chrysler again lifted the curtain of secrecy to show the Pronto Cruiser—a three-door hatch with a retro hot rod styling theme. At the 1999 North American International Auto Show, all the pieces came together in the form of the PT Cruiser,

which married the styling of the Pronto Cruizer with the packaging of the original five-door Pronto.

Eaton best described the PT Cruiser as a "segment buster" at the car's 1999 unveiling. "It could easily be called a flexible activity vehicle, but it's too cool to categorize."

The styling is definitely retro. Round fenders bulge from the front and rear of the car while the coffin-shaped nose contains a large stand-up grille similar to those found on cars of the 1930s. In profile, the PT Cruiser's silhouette resembles that of a Woody or an old sedan delivery.

Starting at an astoundingly low base price of $16,500 including delivery, the PT Cruiser has been a sensation since its launch in April 2000. Built in DaimlerChrysler's Toluca, Mexico, assembly plant, the PT Cruiser is powered by a transversely mounted 150-brake horsepower, 2.4-liter dual-overhead cam (dohc) four-cylinder engine. A European version with a 2.0-liter dohc four will be built in Graz, Austria, a last-minute decision when it was determined that the Toluca plant alone wouldn't be enough to meet North American demand.

Although overall length of the PT Cruiser is about 4 inches shorter than the Neon, its passenger cabin offers nearly the same space as the original short-wheel-base minivan introduced by Chrysler in 1984.

One of the reasons Eaton called the PT Cruiser a "segment buster" is because the vehicle redefines basic proportion in the small-car category. The package itself is unlike any car you've ever driven. The PT Cruiser is much taller, and the H-point (where your hips meet the seat) is much higher than in the Neon. This gives you a command-of-the-road feel normally found in larger trucks, minivans, and sport/utilities. It also gives the PT Cruiser spaciousness and flexibility.

Up front is a pair of bucket seats and in the rear a 35/65 split bench that can be folded forward in two positions or completely removed to reveal a flat load floor. With the rear seat up, the PT Cruiser has a rear storage compartment featuring a multiposition shelf that can be placed in any one of five positions or removed entirely.

The interior displays retro touches, which match the exterior styling. The instruments are housed in three round dials set in a metallic dash plate, and the interior chrome door releases match the chrome door handles on the exterior.

The beauty of the PT Cruiser is that it offers the utility of a minivan without looking like one. It's cool looking and useful at the same time. This unique blend of stand-out styling and an efficient, yet flexible, package

has sent shock waves through an auto industry where small vehicles all looked and acted the same.

"We wanted to provide that same utility and flexibility for people who were interested in something a little more efficient from the package space," said Tom Edson, director of interior systems for the PT Cruiser. "And then the appearance, the sheer magnetism of the style is something. We think there are going to be a lot of people who are in minivan denial attracted to the PT Cruiser. They want the flexibility, they need the space, but the kids are grown up and they don't want to be seen in Mom's minivan anymore."

The PT Cruiser won't be mistaken for Mom's or anyone else's minivan. It's new, it's different, and it's hot.

"I would say that we have an opportunity to define a new market segment, if you will, which is something that doesn't come along very often," said Scott Wilkins, program manager for the PT Cruiser. "Obviously we took elements from other market segments; there are tall cars out there, there are mini-minivans out there. But to be able to put together something recognized as being unique—as being segment busting—was something that just doesn't come along that often."

Nor was it an easy task. The evolution and development of this breakthrough vehicle was a voyage of discovery—a tale of plucky engineers and designers looking to come up with the next big thing. They found it in an all-new kind of small vehicle, a vehicle called the PT Cruiser.

ONE EXPRESSO, PRONTO

It's hard to believe that the PT Cruiser—one of the hottest commodities to ever hit the car market—grew out of a tiny concept car that few took seriously. Even more ironic is the fact that this concept, called the Expresso, was an idea conceived to replace another great American icon, the Checker cab.

It was January 1994 and the Neon had just gone into production. The Expresso was one of a trio of show cars commissioned to demonstrate the flexibility of the Neon sedan and coupe architecture. But few took the Expresso seriously because of the expression that this show car wore. Viewed from the side, the windows had black shades over them like eyebrows, and the door handles were encased in blue "pupils" at the rear corners of the windows, giving the Expresso the appearance that it was "looking" at its own rear wheels.

The Expresso was pure whimsy. But according to DaimlerChrysler Executive Vice President of Product Development and Design Tom Gale, "In a goofy way, the Expresso was a precursor to the tall-roof PT Cruiser."

While the Expresso nominally showcased the Neon platform using the same 132–brake horsepower, 2.0-liter, four-cylinder engine, it actually had a much shorter wheelbase and overall length than Chrysler's newest subcompact. The Expresso rode on a tight 91-inch wheelbase and was only 141.6 inches in overall length. However, the importance of the Expresso wasn't necessarily its compact length, but rather its height. It truly was a tall car. Measuring 69.1 inches in height, it was 15 inches, or well over a foot, taller than the standard Neon.

Producing a tall car opened up a new world for designers conditioned by years of building vehicles that were lower, longer, and wider. The height of the car meant that seating could be upright, which is important in a small car, because it improves visibility by giving the driver a commanding view of the road. By sitting the driver taller in a smaller vehicle, designers also discovered

The Expresso's cartoonish appearance hides the fact that this concept car is a serious study in a new proportion, the tall car, which would pave the way for the PT Cruiser. *John Lamm*

11

Seating inside the Expresso was upright. Adding to the feeling of spaciousness is a minimalist dash. Note the center-mounted instruments. *John Lamm*

The Plymouth Pronto show car was an exercise in developing a flexible, tall-roof vehicle on a subcompact chassis. The Prowler provided the inspiration for the grille. *John Lamm*

that they could reduce the intimidation factor from larger vehicles. Chrysler had found that people felt safer in its minivans not necessarily because of the size of those vehicles, but rather from the higher seating position offered by that vehicle's design.

There were other benefits that flowed from the Expresso's tall profile, chiefly that interior storage capacity increased exponentially. One of the neat features was underseat storage, similar to that found on airplanes. The ease of luggage handling was in fact one of the major criteria driving the Expresso's unorthodox shape.

In profile, the Pronto had very short front and rear overhangs and a tall roof that opened to the sky thanks to a rollback canvas top. *John Lamm*

"When people travel, they pack for a certain mode of transportation," Neil Walling, then vice president of Chrysler advanced design, said at Expresso's launch. "One of the approaches to the interior design of Expresso was to look at the often harried transition from an airplane to a taxi. When you get off an airplane, you have to stuff all your baggage in the trunk of a vehicle that doesn't have any relationship to the one that you just left. It's interesting to us when you design something for specific use, frequently you find that the family usage is also enhanced. The Expresso is simply a more sensible taxi that is also great for families and commuters."

The Expresso represented a paradigm shift in overall vehicle proportion. Unfortunately, because of its cartoonish look, it was difficult at the time to find people who took the car and its precedent-shattering shape seriously. However, the Expresso, dubbed by Chrysler as "the family taxi," was significant because it planted a seed for a new direction in vehicle design. It would yield a change not only in the size of the overall package, but also how this package would be used.

Of note, the Expresso also predicted the use of several technologies that would become commonplace on minivans and cars, such as rear seat entertainment consoles and satellite navigation systems. Even the flexible seating that is an integral part of the PT Cruiser concept could be found here. On the Expresso, the front passenger-side bucket folded flat to allow for additional cargo storage.

While outsiders soon forgot the Expresso, inside Chrysler's advanced design studio the basic vehicle proportions exhibited by this car were definitely on the drawing boards. Work was also in progress on the next-generation Neon and some crucial decisions were about to be made. Would the Neon continue in both coupe and four-door

ONE BOX FITS ALL?

THE PT CRUISER MAY PROVE TO BE THE HOTTEST VEHICLE TO HIT THE AMERICAN market in some time, but the idea of a tall vehicle on a subcompact base doing the work of a minivan has been tried before in the United States—and has failed.

While much of the impetus behind the development of the PT Cruiser has been fueled by the success of small, European, minivanlike vehicles (such as the Renault Megane Scenic and the Opel Zafira), the idea of a tall wagon hails from Japan.

In the early 1980s, Japanese manufacturers experimented with tall-roof wagons built off subcompact cars to increase people- and load-carrying capacities in a country where space is at a premium. Rather than making vehicles longer or wider, they found the room by taking traditional station wagons and literally raising the roof. Sitting more upright takes pressure off legroom while at the same time increases the volume of the passenger compartment. Even more interior room was obtained by reducing the overhang of the nose. This changed the basic proportion of the vehicle from a two-box hood and cabin to a minivanlike one-box or monospace look.

The Dodge Vista, built by Mitsubishi, was one of t
first tall wagons to be sold in the United States.
John Lamm

Among the earliest examples of this new proportion to come to America was Mitsubishi's SSW or Super Space Wagon, which was sold as the Colt Vista by Dodge in 1984 and in later iterations as the Expo by Mitsubishi's U.S. sales arm. A smaller version with a sliding passenger-side rear door was also offered, badged as the Expo LRV and Eagle Summit.

Honda offered a tall wagon in its revamped 1984 Civic line, introducing the tall-roof Shuttle, which also benefited from automatic all-wheel drive. The Shuttle operated primarily in front-drive and would engage the rear wheels only when extra traction was needed. A later variant of the Shuttle was called the WagoVan. The vehicle was eventually dropped from the line, but ironically, the hardware from this model evolved into the popular Honda CR-V, which appeared in 1998. This mini-SUV is also based on the Civic platform and employs the Shuttle's all-wheel-drive technology. But by taking its styling cues from more rugged SUVs, rather than from tamer minivans, the CR-V has turned into a hit for Honda, selling in excess of 50,000 units annually.

Nissan also pioneered the tall-roof market with the Prairie, a 1982 production model based on Nissan's midsize Stanza platform. The boxy Prairie was unique because it offered dual, rear, sliding doors that latched into the trailing edge of the conventional front doors, which meant the vehicle had no B-pillar. It was a feature shared by the more modern-looking Axxess, a 1988 replacement. Once Nissan began marketing its conventional Quest minivan in 1992, the Axxess was quietly dropped from the line.

Nissan's Axxess, which was built off the company
midsize platform, was perceived as too small to b
true minivan and yet suffered from looking too m
like a mom-mobile. *John Lamm*

Even though none of these vehicles became mainstream hits in the United States, customers who did buy them were enthusiastic about the utility and economy they provided. However, most manufacturers are geared toward producing large-volume hits rather than cult classics. No matter how useful these small boxes on wheels were, they just couldn't capture the imagination of American car buyers at large.

The Big Three also eyed this market, but they too were unable to find a design that clicked. "We kept exploring the concept," former Chrysler president Bob Lutz recalled, "but anytime you did a small minivan, no matter how much you disguised it, the American public would say, 'Yeah, interesting interior, right, um, yes. Thank you very much,' and move on." To Lutz, minivans carried the stigma of "mom-mobile." That stigma helped fuel the sales of sport/utilities, which offered the seating capacity and load flexibility of a minivan or station wagon yet projected a rugged, independent image.

One by one, the tall wagons disappeared from U.S. roads, while in Japan, where they are called RVs (Recreational Vehicles), they continue to thrive.

Although the "mini" minivan failed to take root in the United States, Europe was another matter. When Renault revamped its small-car line in 1996, it introduced a monospace tall wagon called the Scenic, which became an instant hit. The Scenic offered more space and features than a comparable subcompact station wagon, with the added allure of a high seating position and a shape that was far more sexy than any minivan. Powered by economical 1.4-, 1.6-, and 2.0-liter gasoline engines and 1.9-liter normally aspirated and turbocharged diesels, the affordable Scenic appealed to a broad range of consumers, from young families to empty nesters. It offered seating for five and tremendous flexibility, thanks to its innovative flip-and-fold seats. The Next Big Thing had arrived in Europe.

The competition responded. Opel launched its version, called the Zafira, in 1999. Powered by 1.6- and 1.8-liter gas engines and 2.0-liter turbodiesels, the Zafira copied the Scenic's high seating position, compact exterior dimensions, and the utility of flip, fold, and removable seating. Opel further upped the ante by offering a seven-passenger version with a pair of third-row jump seats.

Will the idea of a one-box car in the United States work? Early demand for the PT Cruiser was phenomenal because of its unique combination of styling, utility, and pricing. Although Renault doesn't export to the United States and has no plans to market the Scenic through its partner, Nissan, General Motors did look at the idea of selling the Opel Zafira here as a Pontiac; but two problems emerged. The understated look, though attractive for Europeans, won't stand out on American roads. And for about the same price GM would have to charge to make a profit, buyers can have the Montana, a much larger conventional minivan.

The success of SUVs, minivans, and trucks in general has made taller-vehicle proportions much more acceptable to the American buyer as evidenced by the success of the Ford Focus, a subcompact that uses this "taller is better" philosophy. The small one-box vehicle is coming, but it's going to take time, as evidenced by Ford's decision to go back to the drawing boards on a one-box version of the Focus based on the current five-door, because it lacked the third-row seating of the standard-setting Opel Zafira.

For now, the PT Cruiser stands alone in bridging the gap between Europe and the United States in this emerging class of vehicles. Others will follow. But, as has been demonstrated by the vehicles that preceded it, it's going to take styling—and not just packaging—to win over fickle American consumers.

Even though tall wagons failed in the United States, it was the European market that embraced the concept. Renault's Megane Scenic, launched in 1996, was the first of this new generation. *John Lamm*

Opel responded to the Scenic with the Zafira and raised the bar by offering three-row seating for up to seven passengers. *John Lamm*

A large glass hatch opened up the passenger cabin, but in U.S. marketing clinics, consumers didn't feel secure with an exposed cargo area. *John Lamm*

sedan configurations? At one time, a convertible Neon based on the coupe was actually in the works. However, the vehicle had an ungainly look about it, sort of like a bathtub on wheels, and ultimately the idea was abandoned.

With the demise of the ragtop, Chrysler began re-evaluating the necessity of a coupe. If they couldn't make it into a convertible, it became a less appealing proposition. Maybe there was another vehicle archetype, based on the Neon, that would have more flexibility and perhaps spawn a whole new range of vehicles.

"We could have done the replacement Neon four-door and two-door," Gale explained, noting the budget for the all-new model included money for both. "But we said, 'No, we got two bullets to spend. We can't walk away from the four-door. But, okay, why not take the other one and do something different that people are going to pay money for? Everyone else is slugging it out trying to do coupes and we let them do that, while we go over here and do something else.'"

That something else would be a tall car. The public would get a glimpse of what was on Chrysler's mind when the Pronto, a five-door "tall car" concept, was developed in 1996 for unveiling at the January 1997 North American International Auto Show.

The Pronto was designed with a number of objectives in mind, the first and foremost to explore the idea of a small car that could offer the utility of a minivan. It was hoped that such a vehicle would have universal appeal, not only at home, but also in Europe where Chrysler was keen to expand its presence. Pronto also presented an opportunity to experiment with a low-cost plastic-body technology that would enable the company to build small vehicles at a competitive price in the United States.

Pronto's design was modern with just a few retro cues, such as the tall grille opening flanked by almost free-standing bumpers that bore a strong resemblance to the Prowler. The top featured a full-roof, fold-back canvas covering, while at the rear, a large all-glass lift gate was flanked by roof-to-bumper taillamps.

The Pronto had a 101-inch wheelbase and at 148.8 inches in overall length, was about 2 feet shorter than the Neon, and yet at 58 inches, was 2 inches taller.

The interior, which featured front buckets and a rear split fold-down bench, was roomy, practical, and flexible. The instruments were clustered in a single pod in the center of the dash, which accommodated either left- or right-hand drive. The engine was taken from the Neon, a 2.0-liter single-overhead cam (sohc) four that produced 132 horsepower. A three-speed automatic transaxle drove the front wheels. Typical of show cars, the wheel wells were filled with 18-inch alloy rims shod

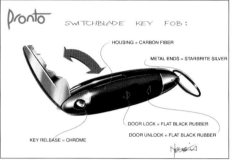

As part of the Pronto styling exercise, designers came up with a unique key fob that resembled a switchblade knife.

with P185/50R-18 tires. The body was made of metal painted a matte finish to simulate composite body skins.

The Pronto Concept called for the use of a composite plastic material called Acrylonitrile/Styrene/Acrylate (ASA), which was essentially a recyclable plastic that could be inexpensively molded and glued together. In addition to eliminating the need for an expensive welding shop, the plastic also featured a molded-in color, which meant no paint shop. By not having to paint the vehicles, assembly would be further simplified and the cost savings would be considerable.

The downside to a plastic body is the fact that people like shiny cars and shiny paint jobs. The dull matte finish was deemed too big a risk on the marketing side and as a result, subsequent takes on the Pronto and PT Cruiser concept would be done in metal with conventional finishes.

Still, what the Pronto concept car was made of was of less import than how it was packaged. "Because of its technology and proportional possibilities, the Plymouth Pronto represents a paradigm-breaking method of changing transportation as we know it," said Neil Walling at the show car's launch. "Pronto gives people space where they need space and economy where they need economy."

When the Pronto concept was unveiled at the Detroit show, it was readily apparent that the European journalists, who were accustomed to the tall-car concept, "got it." They raved about the vehicle's design, the flexibility and roominess of the interior, and the innovative approach to the body panels.

Americans deemed the Pronto "interesting" but felt the matte plastic panels gave the car an unfinished look. They also felt that the large glass hatch lacked security since it allowed anyone to view the contents of the rear cargo area. Despite the subtle Prowler cues, the overall shape of the vehicle, which was fairly crisp and modern, did little to stir the emotions.

"One of the early responses we got from the Pronto was that the concept was a little too conventional in looks and the interior did not live up to the exterior in terms of the promise of utility and spaciousness," said Scott Wilkins, PT Cruiser program manager.

For instance, the shock towers used on the Neon's independent MacPherson strut suspension in the rear pinched into the cargo area. "That research immediately led us to redesign the rear suspension and open up the back end of the vehicle," Wilkins explained.

Chrysler had high hopes that the modern shape with just a hint of Prowler would pique the interest of potential customers to take a closer look at the Pronto. In a way, they were looking for an "inside-out" design, where the attractiveness of what goes on inside the vehicle makes it the primary reason for wanting it, rather than a sexy exterior design.

"What we were aiming to do with the exterior was to bring people in, to attract them to come take a look for whatever reason," Wilkins recalled. "Once they determine that the interior has all this utility and spaciousness, we have them hooked. We can bait them with the exterior but really hook them with the interior, the utility, and the fun-to-use aspects of the vehicle."

Despite the cool reception from American prospects, the Pronto remained an important study because of its groundbreaking approach to small-car proportions. Just as it was discovered with the Expresso, the concept of a high roof allowed for a more-upright passenger seating position, giving the driver the same command-of-the-road seating position found in SUVs and minivans. Until then, it was believed that as people shifted to SUVs, vans, and trucks, small cars would decline in popularity because people couldn't see around the larger vehicles and didn't feel safe. The Pronto was evidence that the answer didn't

"We could have done the replacement Neon four-door and two-door, but we said, 'No, we got two bullets to spend. We can't walk away from the four-door. But, okay, why not take the other one and do something different that people are going to pay money for? Everyone else is slugging it out trying to do coupes and we let them do that, while we go over here and do something else.' "
—Tom Gale

necessarily lie in making small cars larger, but rather they just needed to be taller. Getting the driver and passengers up off the ground not only improves visibility but also the feeling of security.

The package was a winner, but unfortunately the styling wasn't. Chrysler needed not only to bait the customers with the look, it needed to hook them on the spot. The packaging would ice the deal. But, what would it take? The Expresso may have been too funny looking to go into production, while on the other hand, it appeared that the Pronto was way too serious an effort to capture the fancy of those not familiar with the tall-car concept.

"Designs really were not frozen at this point," Wilkins said. After the Pronto was developed, the design office began a serious search for a shape that would get Americans as fired up about the Pronto as the Europeans were. It would not be an easy process.

CHAPTER TWO

GOING RETRO

There's no doubt the essence of the PT Cruiser's phenomenal appeal is its hot rod looks. But within the ranks of Chrysler Corp. there were huge doubts whether the retro look would work with this new type of vehicle, the tall car.

In hindsight, the choice is a clear winner, but keep in mind that decisions concerning the vehicle's design were made back in 1996. Granted, Chrysler did have a series of retro hits with the Dodge Viper, Ram truck, and Plymouth Prowler. It follows, then, that a retro-styled PT Cruiser was a foregone conclusion.

Yet in the mid-1990s no one was sure whether or not retro styling would have staying power. The New Beetle and Audi TT had yet to be introduced. Though the Porsche Boxster concept that debuted in 1995 sported many retro touches echoing the legendary 550 Spyder, the production car greatly muted those cues.

Chrysler's top management and even Tom Gale's design staff were split over the direction that the new car's styling should take. While Gale himself was a huge backer of the Plymouth Prowler, with the PT Cruiser he was more intent on exploring a styling theme that would take Chrysler into the future rather than travel down the retro path. If a shape could be found that would appeal to both American and European sensibilities, it would be a monumental breakthrough in product design.

On the other hand, there was a cadre of executives including then-president Bob Lutz, engineering vice president Francois Castaing, Chris Theodore (who headed the Neon platform development team), and Jim Holden (who was in charge of marketing), who saw a mass-market appeal in the hot rod look.

Lutz, in particular, was becoming frustrated with the design staff's attempts at a breakthrough modern shape. "Every time we had the PT Cruiser discussion, we were back to a look that was similar to the VW Golf, but slightly higher," Lutz recalled.

The final design of the PT Cruiser combines the utility of tall-roof wagons with the rugged good looks of an American hot rod. *John Lamm*

Although the PT Cruiser is tall, the sides have distinct fenders and a rocker panel that recalls a running board. These elements catch light and prevent the vehicle from looking slab-sided. *John Lamm*

Even the designers began to recognize that they had hit a wall in trying to project this breakthrough styling theme.

"We tried this futuristic approach," Gale explained, "and we struggled with it. By the time we finished making that tall package and creating the functionality we wanted, it started to lose something. It wasn't honest to what we were trying to do. We just didn't want to take the image of a minivan and shrink it down. We were trying to find something that would evoke a little different response [than a minivan].

"The more we did the contemporary things, the more it fell into the genre of just a different size of something else," Gale continued. "We wanted to avoid that. Still, we just couldn't make it work. We were really struggling with it."

"Things didn't happen until we started doing this funky retro-style body with the free-standing fenders," said Lutz. "It's amazing nowadays how the free-standing fender theme works. It touches a nostalgia nerve you can't reach in any other way. Think of the Prowler, think of the Ram pickup, and think of the PT Cruiser. It's all getting away from the laid-on-its-side-cereal-box look and getting back to hoods, fenders, and decks. It is not shameful to look at the past."

Still, Gale felt it was important to avoid the temptation to create a straight knock-off of an old car. "We had some things that were absolutely literal 1930s sedan things that Bob Lutz enjoyed—the more literal the better," Gale recalled. "A lot of us were clearly bothered by being quite that literal and we had proportion issues."

Instead, the PT Cruiser merged basic shapes of the 1930s sedan that Lutz liked with more modern forms exhibited by current masters of hot rod design.

The PT Cruiser has a definite forward gesture, or rake, giving it the appearance that it's moving even when standing still. *John Lamm*

"When you look at those fender forms, they're not hand done—they're stampings you never could have done in the late '30s," Gale explained. "And when you look at the resolution of the shape and the way it works with the sill and the way it works with the gesture of the greenhouse, it's what people do today with a hot rod as opposed to what was done with a classic car."

"One of the guys I worked with years ago was named Don Wright," Gale continued. "We tried to come up with things that had this almost underdog emotive feel. One of the things he used to say was, 'Try to make it huggable.' You just want to kind of hug it. Some designs are so alien you just don't want to hug them. I think one of the things we were trying to get at is the fact the PT is a little fun, a little huggable, something you can sidle up to and it's not going to bite you back."

But to get there, Gale needed a design. Enter Bryan Nesbitt, who was then 27 years old. A graduate of the famous Art Center College of Design in Pasadena, California, Nesbitt had worked on the Composite Concept Vehicle (CCV), an entry-level tall car made of composites designed specifically for developing countries.

"We locked him up with the research guys when we were doing the original concept, so he had a great grounding in all the things we were trying to do and we just let him run with it," Gale recalled.

Nesbitt started researching what the public was really looking for in a vehicle like this. The original car he came up with based on that initial research was fairly conventional. The windshield was steeply raked and very carlike. Nesbitt was feeling pressure from the various factions on which way to go. "We found that there were too many cooks involved, too many ideas on the car that prevented us from doing a clear-cut design.

It may look like a panel van when closed, but the PT Cruiser reveals its true mission of carrying both stuff and people when it's opened. *John Lamm*

The nose was a particular challenge for designers who wanted the vehicle to have a strong face while being able to keep the headlamps tucked in tight.
John Lamm

want the rear fenders to bulge out and have the glass inside the line of the wheels," Nesbitt explained. "There's an analogy to a pug dog or a bulldog, where even though they are smaller, they have good stance. Nobody wants to feel vulnerable in these small vehicles, especially with the sea of trucks driving by. The idea of creating the confidence in the car with the surface development was clear from the start."

Nesbitt drew up a final sketch that became the image target. It was a drawing of an orange PT Cruiser that had a radical forward rake to the design. "It was very much a street rod and the one I'd been trying to pull out of him," Gale said. "Lutz was trying to drive us in this really literal direction; others in the company who had one ax to grind or another wanted to go a different way. It was clear it was

"One of the key ingredients to this car was getting as much utility as possible," Nesbitt added. "We were trying to classify the PT Cruiser as a truck with this flat load floor all the way from the back of the front seat to the rear of the vehicle. At the same time we wanted to meet all the car standards for impact and create this hybrid vehicle without looking like a hybrid vehicle."

After a second round of research, Nesbitt came up with a new set of sketches that pursued the retro hot rod theme.

"This is where we got the forward slant of the roof, the bulging fenders, which gave the car a wide stance and a nimble look. The stance of the vehicle is so important—it's a little bit taller so in rear profile you

really going to risk going off track. We had a lot of really harsh discussions and as much as there were always good feelings inside the company, we could always have these frank discussions. I think from a design perspective we struggled with a lot of it. Part of the problem was that it was new territory. There were some similar vehicles out there, but none that looked like this."

To Nesbitt, who wasn't particularly into hot rods to begin with, this approach allowed him to infuse the car with some individuality that he saw lacking in modern cars.

"There seems to be such a spirit in cars from the 1930s, 1940s, 1950s and even 1960s that mirrored the individualism of our culture," Nesbitt observed. "It

Bryan Nesbitt's original design called for a side-hinged door like a sedan delivery. However, a more modern liftgate was settled upon for production. *John Lamm*

seems that in the larger-volume and lower-priced cars of today, that individualism has sort of escaped us. We don't seem to put that type of differentiation into products anymore. My generation missed out on the postwar optimism that funneled into a lot of great products. It seems like that's been gone for awhile and this PT Cruiser hearkens back to that optimism in a way."

But above all, the idea behind the PT Cruiser was to infuse it with a look and functionality that no one else offered.

"From the start, it was exactly what it's supposed to be with no sacrifices in the styling and no sacrifices in the package to get that styling," Nesbitt said.

Creating the right look for the front-drive layout of the PT Cruiser presented Nesbitt with some unique challenges. The key was minimizing the front overhang and paying attention to how the headlamps were positioned.

"I wanted the headlamps as close as possible to the wheels," Nesbitt said. "I didn't want any front overhang that was excessive. When you get into the front-wheel-drive platforms, the engine is hanging over the front of the axle and it usually has a huge front overhang. But I wanted this car to look like it had rear drive, so we straightened the windshield and got its centerline so that you visually see the A-pillar kind of diving right into the wheel."

Aiding Nesbitt in the production of this proportion was the tall engine compartment. By stepping the fenders out from the hood, the surface of the car is broken up. Rather than having a slab-sided, uninteresting vehicle, you have shape—shape that catches light, which in turn actually makes the vehicle look lower. It appears that the fenders and body have been shrink-wrapped around the chassis.

"If you notice, the front end narrows so we get that throwback to the architecture of older vehicles, where we have basically a separate cabin with attached fenders," Nesbitt pointed out. "The surface actually stretches out over the front wheels and then we take the front headlamps and wrap them around the top of

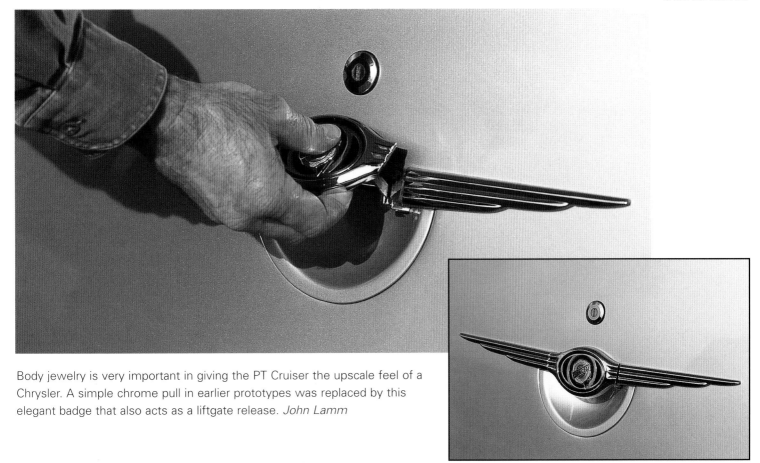

Body jewelry is very important in giving the PT Cruiser the upscale feel of a Chrysler. A simple chrome pull in earlier prototypes was replaced by this elegant badge that also acts as a liftgate release. *John Lamm*

the vehicle and get them as tight as possible, as close to the wheel as possible. This visually shortens the front overhang of the vehicle and it's like pointing a giant arrow at the front tire."

Adding to the effect of a short overhang is the clever use of body color on the fascia up under the front bumper and the use of an offsetting color for the bumpers themselves. This gives the car a little swagger, showing that it is a tough vehicle, not unlike the macho look that has made sport/utility vehicles so popular.

"That's part of the hybrid formula that combines some of the qualities of a car and some of the qualities of a truck," Nesbitt said. "The bumper is shrouded or set back a bit in the fascia so that in side view or when you walk around the vehicle, it gives the impression of a very short front overhang. It appears that the bumpers, as well as the lights, are hugging the front wheels."

In side profile, the wheels are pushed way out to the corners, making the PT Cruiser look both nimble and very stable. The wheel flares give the

DETAILS, DETAILS.

It's not just the styling but the little details that set the PT Cruiser apart from anything else in its price class on the market today. The most obvious touch is the attention paid to body jewelry: the Chrysler winged badge that graces the top of the grille, the chromed door handles and the rear winged badge that doubles as a liftgate release. An earlier iteration used a chrome pull, but a later design nicely integrated the release into the badge itself.

Chrysler paid just as much attention to the lighting. The front headlamps have a faceted appearance thanks to the use of sculpted reflectors for the low and high beams. The turn signals are also used as a design element beneath the large semi-elliptical lens. The taillights are rounded triangles with a surprise. When lit, the lens around the brakelight is round, giving it a bullet-like appearance.

Even inside, little things, like the vents, have a familiar look inspired by the 1950s Fedders air conditioner. The four-spoke steering wheel with its hub detailing, the manual's chrome shifter topped by a cue-ball knob, and the body-colored dash panels pay homage to the American hot rod.
John Lamm

vehicle a muscular look that belies the vehicle's rather modest dimensions.

"I connected those huge fender flares with the door sill. The sill is flared out so it really is a reference to those old running boards that used to connect the front fender to the rear fender," Nesbitt explained. "Another challenge is trying to break up the visual space on the side because we have a taller overall profile. That sill is angled to catch the light. As the sill comes in, it is inset from the fenders and then it flares back out to the width of the car. That surface ends up angling up toward the sun causing it to light up. We end up creating that heritage reference of a running board and at the same time we break up all this surface so it looks interesting."

While Nesbitt was trying to minimize the slab sides of a tall-profile vehicle, he still wanted the vehicle to have a look of substance, which was especially crucial given the hatchback nature of the PT Cruiser.

"We had a lot of research that found that people end up buying Jettas or four-door sedans in the small car market because if you take the overall length of a vehicle and you cap it with a hatch, it just visually looks like a shorter rear overhang." As a result, such a vehicle has less of a visual impact, especially when viewed from the side or rear three-quarters. The remedy on the PT Cruiser was to give the overall shape of the vehicle a forward rake by keeping the beltline high and blacking out the B- and C-pillars to give the roof a chopped appearance. At the same time, the trailing edge of the vehicle also has a bit of forward rake, which gives the vehicle the look of a longer rear overhang without actually having one.

Meanwhile, on the hatch itself, the rear window is small and placed high, minimizing the view into the cargo compartment, which offers the owners more of a sense of security. In addition, with the rear of the vehicle taller than the front, the second row of seats is mounted slightly higher, theater-style, giving the back-seat occupants a better view out the front windshield. "It also gives the PT a certain attitude, as though it can hold its

The winged Chrysler badge now adorns the nose of the PT Cruiser, which was originally conceived as a Plymouth. *John Lamm*

Large, clear lenses and a multi-element front headlamp assembly add to the jeweled look of the PT Cruiser's nose. *John Lamm*

own—a little street-smart attitude," Nesbitt said.

Gale believes that the blacked-out pillars give the PT Cruiser a more modern appeal and that body-colored pillars would have made the vehicle's profile look too retro.

"When you look at how the body is resolved in terms of the upper body structure, it would have been a lot more overt if we had left body color pillars and things like that," Gale said. "But we went back for a clean, open, and gestured—almost hardtop—look, where the pillars went black.

"The one thing that really helps us pull this off is that wheel-to-body relationship," Gale continued. "The PT has a great stance. It's very capable, it looks like it's got the ability to do things, and is very much a modern-day car in function as opposed to a hot rod. That stance comes from planting the wheels way outside the glass plane. All of a sudden, you don't have a van shape—minivans typically have the wheels on the same plane as the side glass. What we did was keep the wheels outside the plane of the glass to give it the full fender flare shapes, while still maintaining a relatively spacious cabin."

Gale said the PT Cruiser has the same feel as a Legends racer, a series of small spec racers powered by motorcycle engines. Charlotte Motor Speedway impresario Humpy Wheeler developed these scaled-down competition cars in the early 1990s as a

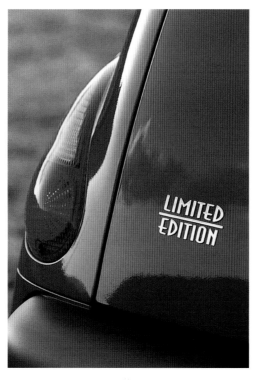

"I think one of the things we were trying to get at is the fact the PT is a little fun, a little huggable, something you can sidle up to and it's not going to bite you back."—*Tom Gale*

low-cost spec racing series. The cars themselves were scaled-down replicas of late-1930s stock cars.

The full fender look has other advantages. The flares in the rear allow for minimal wheelwell intrusion in the passenger cabin, which creates a good load space.

"Anytime we had the more contemporary solutions where you have the wheel and glass planes converge or, heaven forbid, the glass plane gets outside the wheels, you lose this look of stability," Gale asserted. "We just didn't want that. This has got to have the look of stability. It's one of those things I don't think people can verbalize, but they know it when they see it."

One interpretation of the PT Cruiser is that it is sort of a small sedan delivery, those panel-sided trucks that delivered everything from bread to flowers.

"If you look at Bryan's original sketch, it really started out as a sedan delivery," Gale pointed out. "We even looked at one point in time at having a [rear] door hinged from the side, but it didn't work, so we went back to the hatch and I'm glad we did. As you walk around the car, it's got a slant-back look to it."

The key here, according to Gale, is to stay away from the classic form of a station wagon or a minivan

Even the model markings, such as this Limited Edition, are done in chrome to add value not usually seen on entry-level vehicles. *John Lamm*

Plastic bezels around the instruments are painted body color to give the retro look of a metal interior. White faces on the instruments help reflect light, while the graphics on the gauges have an Art Deco feel. *John Lamm*

where the hatch actually has a curve to it in an attempt to maximize cargo volume.

"With the PT we said we're going to make it kind of flat or with a slant-back feel to it," Gale said. "Also, we wanted to keep the bumper relatively low, which changes the proportion and improves the functionality with its low liftover height."

Another area that paid huge dividends was the attention to detail when it came to badge and exterior jewelry. The door handles, for instance, are old-fashioned chrome handles with buttons. The winged Chrysler badge on the nose is an elegant piece of trim. The hatch release, which originally was just a chrome pull with a button, was later reworked to be part of the rear badging.

Similar attention to small details in the execution of the interior would prove crucial to the success of the overall design.

"The interior is really where I think in a way it keeps the promise of the outside," Gale noted. "After all,

The passenger-side dash is also body-colored. This plastic insert actually hides the airbag. *John Lamm*

the vehicle functionally started with the interior, not the outside. It started with the package."

That package began with the driver feeling that he or she is in control, and has command of the road. It's a feeling that many have experienced in minivans and sport/utility vehicles, but never before in something the size of a PT Cruiser.

A high seating position allows the driver to look through the back of the vehicle in front of him or her to see what's going on up ahead. The height of the PT

Cruiser allowed the designers to do that. The seats have a more chairlike feel to them and the taller roof allows the front and rear seats to be positioned much closer to each other without losing legroom because the occupants are sitting more upright. That in turn allows for more space in the back and the PT Cruiser's remarkable ability to carry an 8-foot ladder or a two-by-eight piece of wood with the rear hatch closed.

There's no question that this sort of flexibility would win over customers. The challenge then was to create

37

The center stack has a conventional, modern appearance that blends well with the retro touches. Note the steering wheel with its small hub. Originally, the PT Cruiser was to share its wheel with the redesigned Neon. *John Lamm*

an interior environment that supported the imagery on the outside, as well as make provisions for such technical matters as placement of airbags and the possibility of left- and right-hand drive.

That job was left to a dedicated team of interior designers led by Jeff Godshall, an acknowledged authority and author on vintage cars. He was the perfect choice for someone charged with combining a modern interior with the same kind of heritage cues found on the exterior design.

That doesn't mean a vehicle with the flexibility of the PT Cruiser didn't have its own unique challenges. It did mean he had to approach the design from a different perspective. The traditional approach is "a place for

Dash vents were designed to resemble outlets found on 1950s air conditioners.
John Lamm

Cruiser promised a different vehicle, so we went through a number of different iterations of what we might do for the interior. One idea was an instrument panel with great big removable speakers at either end giving it a sort of boombox kind of look. Then we did one where we had a couple of concave shapes with instruments sitting on pods inside these concave openings. But the public thought the pods looked a little fragile and if you bumped them they might go out of adjustment."

The designers also looked at putting the main instrument cluster in the middle, similar to the original Pronto concept. It would be an easy solution for both left-and right-hand-drive configurations. "We didn't think it was appropriate," Godshall said, alluding to the fact that cheap cars from the 1950s, especially those coming from right-hand-drive countries, used this approach.

Finally, Godshall hit on the idea of creating a symmetrical instrument panel. It was a look consistent with hot rods, which were the inspiration for the exterior. "In those types of cars, that's the way panels were done; they were symmetrical. It might have the speedometer on one side matching the clock on the other."

In the PT Cruiser, Godshall put the instruments in three little tunnels with a chrome ring surrounding each of the instruments. Originally, the instruments had black faces, but because of the depth of the tunnels, it

everything and everything in its place." But to Godshall, the PT Cruiser's flexible interior features meant "the 'everything in its place' principle quickly became more of a 'duffel bag' philosophy. With a duffel bag, you place things inside any way you want. You control how much goes in and how it's all configured. The PT Cruiser is all about that type of flexibility."

Still, he knew that no matter how contemporary the function of the interior, the appearance had to be consistent with the exterior shape.

"One of the aesthetic functions on the interior of an automobile or any product is to express the ambiance of the exterior," Godshall explained. "There has to be a link there when you open the door. You've got to fulfill the promise made by the exterior. The exterior of the PT

was switched to white faces to make them easier to read.

Another element playing into the retro theme was bringing the exterior color into the interior. Both sides of the dash would mirror the exterior color and mimic the kind of painted metal finish found in older vehicles.

Along with the use of exterior colors on the interior, Godshall said a circular theme to the instruments and vents began to evolve.

"We have the three circular instruments, and we have the circular air-conditioning outlets on each end of the cluster and airbag door. And then there are the circular vents on the center stack," Godshall said. "We were able to nicely integrate them and then put the power window switches in the middle, and the whole thing really came out very well, I thought."

Originally the PT Cruiser was slated to use the 2000 Neon steering wheel, but once the group received

the first mockup panels and put the Neon steering wheel in front of it, they decided the new four-spoke wheel didn't scale well to the dashboard. The airbag horn pad was way too big and obscured the unique styling of the PT Cruiser dash. Engineering looked at the wheel, agreed, and found some money for a new steering wheel that had a much smaller, round hub that still packaged an airbag and was consistent in look to the round gauges and air-conditioning outlets.

"That was the smallest hub we could get and still get the airbag inside," Godshall recalled.

When it came time to design the manual gearshift, the team developed a sketch of a knob that had a tall boot, Godshall said. It looked cool in the sketches, but when the model came back, "It sort of looked like a token from a Parker Brothers board game," Godshall laughed. "I had engineers coming to me saying, 'You're

Bryan Nesbitt's original sketch for the PT Cruiser looks more like a sedan delivery than a pure hot rod. Note the exposed B- and C-pillars, which give the vehicle a more retro look. *Chrysler*

not going to do that, are you?' We showed it to Trevor Creed, our vice president, and he asked why couldn't we do something a little more retro . . . what about a cue ball kind of thing? Again that wasn't in the program. We showed it to the appropriate people in engineering and by golly we got it."

According to Gale, it's touches like these and attention to detail that are absolutely crucial in provoking a response from potential customers.

"It is very intentional," Gale said. "We discovered this with the Ram pickup truck and our other products. We want to create an emotional reaction, one that people either love or hate.

"An emotional reaction leads to an emotional attachment to that vehicle. It is something they remember and it is something significant. That emotional reaction then becomes value to the product; it becomes value to the customer. And it becomes an identifier with our brand.

"To me, it's a testament to the original process in which we recognized that we only have so much money and we decided what was the best car we could do," Gale said. He added, surprisingly, that it's not so much about the design but rather what the whole vehicle says. "To me it has nothing to do with the styling. It's more a matter of where's the emotional reaction. If you go into the market and you don't have that emotion that builds equity, then what are you inventing? Increasing the equity in the small-car niche can be valuable. And that's going to create more value and satisfy the customer. This isn't just frivolous, the next hot thing. This is something that is lasting and has real value to it."

This early sketch suggests an extreme forward gesture, or rake, to the design, resulting in an aggressive attitude. *Chrysler*

A later version of the PT Cruiser shows the blacked-out B- and C-pillars, which provided a much cleaner look. *Chrysler*

CHAPTER THREE

CRUIZE CONTROL

If going retro is the way to sell what is essentially a European-sized package to Americans, will Europeans be willing to buy a truly American-looking vehicle?

It was a question that needed to be answered, since the idea behind the PT Cruiser was to sell it globally. But, the track record of U.S. manufacturers selling products produced at home to Europeans has been pretty dismal. American cars are generally derided as being too big, too soft, and too inefficient. On top of it, Chrysler had little or no brand equity left abroad for its cars. Instead, it was rebuilding its reputation with trucks, principally Jeeps and minivans.

But rather than being a weakness, this was found to be the PT Cruiser's strength.

"The perception is that when you're buying a Chrysler worldwide, you are buying an American vehicle," Bryan Nesbitt said. "We wanted to reregister that this vehicle is coming from America, that this is Detroit sheet metal. In America itself we wanted to create this identity. It was important in the small-car market where everybody has the same suppliers, the same size, and the same price, and they all look the same. We really wanted to break that mold to create a new car."

The PT Cruiser needed a hook and that hook was nostalgia. It would be American nostalgia that would appeal to buyers everywhere.

"We see this in other areas," Nesbitt explained. "If you take Old Navy, for example. This new store franchise created equity by tapping into nostalgia with the actual brand itself. In a way, the PT Cruiser does the same thing by capitalizing on our heritage. We've been making cars for a long time, but maybe the world doesn't realize it."

Part of that heritage is the iconoclasm associated with the hot rod movement. It has the same type of universal appeal that made Elvis Presley, blue jeans, and Coca-Cola worldwide phenomenons.

"If we look at American automotive heritage, it's the hot rod that is really the epitome of that individualism of

The Pronto Cruizer was built to test the retro approach on European prospects. This three-door show car had a longer hood and more exaggerated features than the production car. *Bill Delaney*

that character," Nesbitt explained. "And so in the automotive arena, to tap into and capitalize on the hot rod feel is kind of a celebration of that individualism. And that's what the PT Cruiser is, a celebration. You want to recognize that no matter where you are, this is a Chrysler—it's an American car and there is no question that there wouldn't be any other manufacturer besides Chrysler that would do it. It could only be us. Think of it as looking forward by looking backward."

The key to making this image work is the package itself. Even though American cars are smaller and more efficient than they were 20 years ago, the average U.S.-built car is still considered huge overseas. And then there is the price of fuel, which is four times higher outside the United States. Other than specialized vehicles such as Jeeps and minivans or even some luxury cars, there is little demand in Europe for the "average" American car. Conversely, there is little appeal in America for the "average" European car, which is a small hatchback vehicle.

"It's ironic that Volkswagen sells more Jettas, a traditional-looking sedan with a trunk, than hatchback Golfs over here," said Nesbitt. "Nobody aspires to a hatchback vehicle unless it's jacked off the ground and has an expensive four-wheel-drive system underneath it or it's a minivan. Hatchbacks just don't sell well in the States. The profile doesn't sell well. And yet they're very efficient. So why is that? Why do we have that discrepancy?

"People want all the utility, but the vehicle had better not look utilitarian," Nesbitt said. With the hot rod look of the PT Cruiser, he believes that they have solved the conundrum of making a hatchback that will appeal to Americans and an American small car that will appeal to Europeans.

"I think it will be great," Nesbitt said, explaining, "You know when you're going to a Gap store overseas

The interior, despite such up-to-date features as a computer screen with onboard navigation, is decidedly Art Deco. *Bill Delaney*

"If we look at American automotive heritage, it's the hot rod that is really the epitome of that individualism, of that character. And so in the automotive arena, to tap into and capitalize on the hot rod feel is kind of a celebration of that individualism. And that's what the PT Cruiser is, a celebration."
—*Bryan Nesbitt*

because it's like walking into Cowboyville. It's things like Levi jeans and the mythology behind America that is fulfilled over there."

But even before going into production, Chrysler needed to test the theory that Europeans would accept a new hatchback vehicle with a decidedly American twist to the exterior design.

As work was progressing on the five-door PT Cruiser (code-named PT44), the time came to try another concept car out on the public. This time, the show car would have two missions—first, to experiment with the hot rod styling theme in the European market, and second, to confuse the competition, making them think the company was headed in a different direction.

The concept car commissioned for the 1998 Geneva Motor Show was called the Pronto Cruizer, establishing a direct link to the original Pronto show car. It marked only the second time that a Chrysler show car had debuted in Europe, the first being the Portofino at Frankfurt more than a decade earlier. It was also decided to make the Pronto Cruizer a three-door hatchback (the curveball for the competition), even though

At the Pronto Cruizer's launch during the 1998 Geneva Auto Show, the cover story was that the vehicle was primarily built to showcase new 1.4- and 1.6-liter engines that were being jointly developed by Chrysler and BMW. *John Lamm*

the PT44 was being developed as a five-door. By debuting the car in Geneva as a three-door, Chrysler's cover story was that it was developing a tall-car variation of the Neon, but it was only doing it for the European market. The company wanted to keep the five-door concept and the fact that it would be geared primarily for the U.S. market, under wraps.

At the time, Neil Walling, who headed Chrysler's advance design, said the Pronto Cruizer's brief was to "showcase our joint venture engine with BMW, a 1.6-liter four cylinder." BMW and Chrysler had an arrangement to build that 115-horsepower engine along with a 1.4-liter unit in South America for use primarily in European markets.

As a three-door, the Pronto Cruizer could be viewed as Chrysler's answer to Volkswagen's New Beetle. It offered styling cues that were uniquely American with the kind of features that Europeans had come to expect from cars in this class. In other words, rather than showing off a potential rival to the Renault Megane Scenic, the quintessential mass-market tall car, Chrysler seemed to be serving up a cult car with styling heavily influenced by American pop culture.

"American design has some interesting roots," Walling says, referring to the history of the hot rod. "Some of it was bad; some of it was really bad. But a lot of it was good. This Cruizer could only come from our culture."

The Pronto Cruizer, unlike the plastic-body Pronto proposal, was intended from the start to be a steel unit-body vehicle. The Cruizer, also penned by Nesbitt, rode on the Neon's 104-inch platform, but at 167.2 inches was nearly 5 inches shorter. It was also 4 inches taller.

The PT Cruizer, a five-door evolution of the Pronto Cruizer show car, was a surprise addition at the 1999 North American International Auto Show. Though less aggressive than the three-door, the PT Cruizer show car featured a canvas rollback top, a larger 2.4-liter four-cylinder engine, and all-wheel drive. *John Lamm*

Within minutes of revealing the PT Cruizer concept, the wraps were taken off the PT Cruiser production car. Painted silver, this version was front-drive, sported gray bumpers instead of body-colored bumpers, and was set for production just 14 months later. *John Lamm*

Nesbitt's early sketch of the three-door Pronto Cruizer suggests a three-window coupe. Note the side exhausts. *Chrysler*

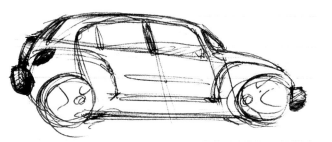

One of the early sketches of the PT Cruiser shows a more conventional greenhouse theme and angular wheel-house treatment. *Chrysler*

The final sketch of the Pronto Cruizer, though still striking, has a more conservative ground clearance and more of a hatchback appearance. *Chrysler*

An alternate proposal had a conventional passenger-car roofline taken directly from the Neon with a more modern approach, as demonstrated by the squared-off fender flares, rectangular headlamps, and conventional grille opening. *Chrysler*

Again, as a concept car, it had an aggressive wheel and tire package: The fronts were 18x7-inch wheels with P205/55R-18 tires, while the rears were 19x7.5-inch rims with P215/55R-19 rubber.

The huge four-wheel disc brakes were taken from the Viper, while the MacPherson strut suspension at all four corners came directly from the Neon, along with the five-speed manual transmission.

Nesbitt said the proportions exhibited by the Pronto Cruiser were spot-on for Europe. "Tall cars have a lot more personality and the high beltline gives the car a protective quality, which is something that you see in European hatchbacks. Their cars may be small, but they give you, through large side surfaces, the feel of being secure."

Painted a color called Aztek Gold, the Pronto Cruiser had an exaggerated look to it. The cab was set back, the fenders and grille seemed larger than life, and the running boards, which flow smoothly into the fenders, were a distinct 1940s styling cue. The roof sported a fold-back canvas sunroof. A steeply raked rear hatch and larger rear wheels made the car look like it was ready to pounce.

Complementing Nesbitt's exterior work was an interior that blended both Art Deco and techno touches. According to Dave Smith, a 10-year Chrysler veteran and graduate of Detroit's Center for Creative Studies, he was striving for a look that was unlike Japanese interiors, which focus on gadgetry. "This has a European feel—functional, not trendy."

The rear of the more conventional approach retained the large glass hatch of the Pronto show car. It was a feature that didn't go over well in U.S. clinics where participants felt it made the cargo area less secure. *Chrysler*

Once a more retro approach was decided upon, things started falling into place. This sketch shows an effort to offset the extreme forward gesture with a more upright rear liftgate, inspired by early surf wagons—panel deliveries and woodies. *Chrysler*

An aluminum finish was used on all functional interior areas, including the instrument cluster, armrest, center stack, door handles, steering wheel, shifter knob, and shifter gate. Carbon fiber was used on items such as the door map pockets, and the leather seat texture had a unique carbon fiber look to it.

The instruments were clustered in a pod behind the retro-styled three-spoke steering wheel with light blue–colored faces. When the headlights were on, the instruments were bathed in a deep blue light. A screen for the on-board navigation system dominated the center stack and three simple knobs controlled the heating and air conditioning system. In a light touch, the shift ball and the pedals were decorated with "happy faces."

The car was a hit at Geneva, though some British journalists sniffed that the look was somewhat similar to the legendary London Taxi. But more important, everyone who saw the Pronto Cruizer as an American hot rod retromobile "got it."

The misdirection employed at Geneva had its desired impact. Even though Chrysler continued to test heavily disguised mules of the PT Cruiser, it had successfully planted a seed of doubt on what types of vehicles were involved in the project. Many in the industry assumed that it would be a Europe-only three-door hatchback.

There was yet one more concept car in the works, called the PT Cruizer, which would be shown to the public before the production PT Cruiser was unveiled. More conservative looking than the Pronto Cruizer, the PT Cruizer had five doors. The grille and fenders were more restrained and the touchdown point of the windshield was much farther forward. In addition, both the front windshield and rear hatch were less steeply raked, and yet the overall vehicle retained some of the forward-thrusting gesture of the Geneva show car. Best of all, there was no mistaking the hot rod influence in the car's styling.

Painted the same Aztek Gold color as the Pronto Cruizer, the PT Cruizer also shared the same full-roof

CHRYSLER PT CRUISER

Very early in the project, as this sketch demonstrates, a panel van was also on the table. *Chrysler*

The approach of a symmetrical theme with round instruments set deep on the driver's side was ultimately selected. *Chrysler*

One of the alternate interiors had the instruments clustered beneath a brow on the dash. In clinics, participants felt the design would be too fragile in everyday use. *Chrysler*

roll-back canvas top. But mechanically, the PT Cruiser was quite different. It was equipped with a 2.4-liter four-cylinder engine producing 150 horsepower. And that engine was mated to an all-wheel-drive system.

The PT Cruiser was set for a surprise launch at the 1999 North American International Auto Show. The press had been briefed ahead of time about Chrysler's four concept cars, but nothing was said about the PT Cruiser. An elaborate stage was constructed where the four concepts, the Dodge Charger, Dodge Power Wagon, Chrysler Citadel, and Jeep Commander, would be rolled out on stage, put into a "time machine," and a date would pop up with the calendar year showing when such a vehicle would be feasible.

When Chairman Bob Eaton had gone through the four concepts, he announced that there was yet another car. Out rolled the PT Cruiser. The car was rolled into the time machine and the date 2000 flashed. Out popped another car, this one silver. It was called the PT Cruiser and represented the production version that would go on sale in March 2000.

The interior carried on the Art Deco theme of both the Pronto Cruizer and the PT Cruiser. The instrument panel used two body-colored plastic inserts with a painted metal-looking finish on the dash front. The passenger-side insert hid the airbag, while the driver's side had three instrument faces with chrome bezels set into it. The center stack also had a metallike finish. On the manual-equipped PT Cruiser, the shifter was a chrome lever with a Bakelite knob, adding to the car's retro cues.

Like the Megane Scenic it was to compete with in Europe, the PT Cruiser had a flexible seating system. The rear seats folded down or could easily be removed, while the front passenger seat folded flat forward, allowing objects as long as 8 feet to be carried inside the vehicle. A unique five-position parcel shelf in the back could be used to divide the cargo area behind the rear seat or even propped out the back with a drop-down leg as a table for use at tailgate parties.

The only discernable differences between the PT Cruiser show car and the PT Cruiser production model were the latter's gray bumpers and lack of a sunroof and all-wheel-drive system. While the simultaneous launch of concept car and production version was an industry first, it was the production model that got all the ink as most show reports overlooked the gold all-wheel-drive concept.

It was a long way from an idea that started out as the Plymouth Pronto and ended up the Chrysler PT Cruiser, a journey that also foreshadowed the demise of the Plymouth nameplate. The finished car, while using the Prowler-inspired grille and promising to sell for a Plymouth-like base price of around $16,000, used chromed door handles and the ornate Chrysler winged badge front and rear to convey a much more upscale aura. The PT Cruiser was for real and it was on its way.

CHAPTER FOUR

UNDER THE PT CRUISER'S SKIN

The uniqueness of the PT Cruiser isn't limited to its shape. How all the mechanical bits came together for this groundbreaking vehicle shows how much you can do with a few common components and a lot of hard work.

One misconception is that the PT Cruiser is merely a reskinned Neon. Nothing can be further from the truth when you look at a comparison of base vehicles. The Neon rides on a 103-inch wheelbase and is 185 inches in overall length. It is powered by a 2.0-liter sohc 134–brake horsepower four offered with a choice of five-speed manual or three-speed automatic. It also has a fully independent suspension.

The PT Cruiser also has a 103-inch wheelbase, but is only 168.8 inches in overall length. It does have a base 2.0-liter dohc four-cylinder engine that makes 140 brake horsepower, but that's for export only. In the United States, PT Cruisers are equipped with 2.4-liter dohc four-cylinder engines that make 150 brake horsepower

and are offered with a five-speed manual or a four-speed automatic. The PT's rear suspension is a beam axle, as opposed to an independent setup, to increase the load-carrying capacity.

Inside, the PT Cruiser has an interior volume of 120.2 cubic feet, which actually puts the vehicle in the EPA's large-car class. This large space translates to generous front head and legroom of a respective 40.4 and 40.6 inches, while shoulder room measures 54.6 inches and hip room 54 inches. The front seats have 9 inches of fore/aft travel. In the rear, headroom is 39.6 inches, primarily because the rear seats are stepped up theater-style to improve the visibility of back-seat passengers. Legroom is 40.8 inches, shoulder room is 53.9 inches, and hip room is 46.8 inches. When the rear seat is up there's 19 cubic feet of cargo space, which grows to 64.2 cubic feet when the rear seats are removed.

The PT Cruiser owes much of its spaciousness to its height. It stands 63 inches tall, which is 7 inches taller

Although the PT Cruiser was developed out of funds and engineering talent devoted to the 2000 Neon, very few components are shared between the two. *Chrysler*

than the Neon, or just 3 inches shy of your average mini-van, making it quite a different animal. And yet, the PT Cruiser owes its existence and much of its cost savings to Chrysler's entry-level four-door sedan. First off, the money to create the PT Cruiser came from the allocation for the 2000 Neon platform. Second, the PT Cruiser resides with the small-car platform team. Many of the same engineers who helped develop the new Neon also worked on the PT Cruiser. And finally, where possible, component sets such as the five-speed manual, the front suspension, and other assorted bits and pieces that could be shared were used in order to cut costs.

"There is a synergy between the Neon and PT Cruiser," said Dan Knott, director of vehicle development for the small-car platform. "It's not so much that the vehicles are the same or that these vehicles share so many parts. Rather, it's sharing the process, and what we learned on the Neon we were able to apply to the PT Cruiser."

But the challenges in packaging and building the PT Cruiser were different and much more difficult than the development of, say, a passenger car or even a mini-van. Much of the challenge lay in the shape of the PT Cruiser. The passenger cabin is large and boxy like a minivan, while the nose of the vehicle is very narrow and tall with a short front overhang. While those dimensions give the PT Cruiser its one-of-a-kind look, packing all the underhood components in that space was new territory for the engineers.

The engines themselves had already been developed for other products in the company's line. Export versions of the PT Cruiser are equipped with 2.0-liter (1,995-cc) dohc 16-valve four-cylinder engines that produce 140 horsepower at 5,700 rpm and 139 ft-lb of torque at 4,150

The biggest engineering challenge was finding a way to fit the 2.4-liter four-cylinder engine in the narrow engine bay. *John Lamm*

rpm. These engines are equipped with electronically controlled sequential multiport fuel injection, and use cast-iron blocks with aluminum heads. The engine is redlined at 6,752 rpm on manual models and 6,720 on automatics and has a compression ratio of 9.6:1. This is the same 2.0-liter engine that has seen duty on base Dodge Stratus sedans equipped with five-speed manuals.

The engine used in the North American market is the larger 2.4-liter (2,429-cc) dohc 16-valve four. It also has a cast-iron block with an aluminum head, and it produces 150 horsepower at 5,500 rpm and 162 ft-lb of torque at 4,000 rpm. Engine speed is electronically limited to 6,240 rpm and the compression ratio is 9.4:1. Fuel is delivered through an electronically controlled sequential multiport injection system. This engine also employs counter-rotating balance shafts for smoother operation.

Both engines feature new catalytic-converter technology that enables the 2.4-liter engine to meet Low Emission Vehicle (LEV) and Ultra Low Emission Vehicle (ULEV) standards as well as European Stage 3 requirements. These advancements include low-mass exhaust manifolds made of lightweight, thin-wall cast iron, which helps speed catalytic converter warm-up. The converter itself is mounted closer to the exhaust manifold resulting in quicker light off. Also enabling the converter to get up to operational temperatures more quickly are the new 600-cell-per-square-inch substrates. More cells provide more area exposed to the passing exhaust gases and ensure more complete burning of hydrocarbons and other pollutants.

The engines are mated to a choice of five-speed manual or four-speed automatic transaxles. The five-speed synchronized manual uses a cable-operated three-plane shifter, while the input shaft is stiffer, the gear facings wider, and the bearings stronger than the Neon's manual. Fourth and fifth gears are overdrive with respective ratios of 0.971 and 0.811. Final drive is 3.94.

The automatic is electronically controlled with fully adaptive shifting and improved torque management for

Seatbelts are integrated into the seats to make removing and installing the seats easier. Even the center passenger on the rear bench has a three-point belt. *John Lamm*

quick shifts. The interactive speed control and engine and transaxle controllers interact to prevent the transaxle from hunting between third and fourth gears in hilly terrain. The automatic is equipped with direct drive in third and a 0.69 ratio for overdrive fourth. Effective final drive is 3.91 with the 2.4-liter engine and 4.07 with the 2.0-liter powerplant.

Scott Wilkins, PT Cruiser program manager, said the 134-horsepower 2.0-liter sohc four from the Neon was initially considered. "In taking a look at the size of the vehicle, the projected weight of the vehicle [which was 3,200 pounds], we felt that we wanted to have a bit more spunk and sportiness to it than the 2-liter would probably deliver," he said.

"We knew the car was going to be heavier than a Neon, so we started looking at packaging the 2.4-liter right at that point in time. Later on we added the four-

UNDER THE PT CRUISER'S SKIN

A twist-beam rear axle with Watts linkage was used instead of a more conventional independent rear with MacPherson struts. This approach eliminated the rear shock towers and opened up the cargo bay.
John Lamm

Neon originally was slated to donate its steering wheel to the PT Cruiser. However, a different design was eventually used. *Chrysler*

speed automatic transmission instead of doing the three-speed from the Neon. It turned out to be an excellent powertrain choice for the North American markets. And we still have the 2-liter, which is technically just less than 2 liters [1,995 cc] to help us in the export markets where displacement is a tax issue.

"The real packaging trick was placing that 2.4-liter engine in the engine compartment," he continued. "We did everything between the rails of a relatively narrow vehicle with very short front overhang. So we had to

develop the engine package from scratch."

While the PT has a narrower nose than the Neon sedan, it is not quite as stubby as a mini-van's. The engineers found additional room in the height of the engine compartment.

"We developed an all-new intake manifold," Wilkins explained. "The engine itself stands up taller than the engine would in a minivan, for example. So, while the base engine is the same as the mini-van, there were a lot of modifications to the intake manifold induction system to take advantage of the PT Cruiser's tall engine compartment."

The power rack-and-pinion steering, which has an 18:1 ratio and moves three turns lock-to-lock, also had to fit in relatively tight quarters.

"I wouldn't say it was a nightmare," Wilkins laughed. "But I do think the engineers who were working on it initially had night-mares about trying to get their components in. The packaging space is very, very, very tight. We always get a kick out of those responding to photos on the Web site who ask when it's going to get a V-8. It's difficult enough to get the four-cylinder in there."

Ironically, one component set from the Neon that worked quite well with the PT Cruiser package was the front independent MacPherson strut suspension. "The front suspension itself is architecturally similar to the Neon," Wilkins said. "We obviously were looking at doing it as inexpensively as possible, and we tried to

As part of the development process, early PT Cruisers were tested in Europe. At right is one of the competitive vehicles brought along for analysis, an Opel Zafira. *Chrysler*

During a stop at a European gas station, Chrysler engineers give another tall car, the Fiat Multipla (center), the once-over. *Chrysler*

A completely redesigned intake system, needed to be developed to fit the 2.4-liter four in the cramped engine bay. *Chrysler*

maintain the same architecture if not the exact components from one vehicle to the next. We knew the characteristics of the Neon suspension, we knew how it would perform, and it was a matter of only changing the tuning in the case of the front suspension."

Part of that tuning was developing a "low-lean" geometry, which helps reduce body roll in corners. A stiff front suspension cross-member attaches the front suspension to the body, which in addition to providing excellent lateral support, provides a firm base for the attachment of the steering rack.

"This stiffness, which results in a high natural vibration frequency, helps limit the transmission of road noise and engine vibration to the interior," Knott said.

While this layout worked well up front, a different approach was used at the rear of the car. Going back to the Pronto show car, the engineers knew they would have a problem if they tried to carry over the stock Neon's MacPherson strut independent rear. The shock towers for that suspension would greatly intrude into the cargo area, thereby reducing the utility

of the overall package. A different approach was needed. Independent rear suspensions are generally viewed as superior when it comes to vehicle handling, yet it was recognized that the PT Cruiser's forte would be the way it handled people and cargo rather than the road.

"Our objective was then to look for a way to put as much of the suspension under the floor as possible and open up the back right to the wheelwell," Wilkins explained. "We did that by basically going back to some earlier types of suspensions, the beam axle that we know very well from earlier passenger cars as well as minivans."

The transverse beam axle causes the tires to remain perpendicular to the road during cornering, which enhances handling even when carrying a full complement of cargo. The rear suspension's coil springs and jounce stops mount above the beam in line with the wheel centerline, to prevent after-shake when the wheel hits a bump.

But the PT Cruiser would use the beam axle with a twist. In addition to the usual trailing arms locating the rear axle to the vehicle, the engineers used a lateral suspension device, called a Watts linkage, to control lateral movement of the axle. The Watts linkage consists of two transverse links that pivot from the outer edge of the body, which connect to a third link at the inboard end. This third link pivots at its center on the axle and moves vertically relative to the body. The linkage reduces lateral movement of the axle, allowing the wheelwells to be thinner, induces less side-to-side variation in handling, and helps to distribute

This is a computer model of the 150-horse-power 2.4-liter powerplant. *Chrysler* transverse loads more evenly for precise handling. By distributing these loads, the Watts linkage also reduces stress on the body structure and allows for the use of softer bushings, which helps ensure a smooth, more comfortable ride.

The large, boxy passenger cabin presented a challenge to the structural engineers when it came to meeting safety standards. The removable seats and parcel shelf meant additional bracing had to be built into the floor and roof of the PT Cruiser in order to create a body rigid enough to sustain impacts.

"What you do," said Ernie Laginess, director of body engineering for the small-car platform, "is add more structure to the floor and into the side of the vehicle to replace some of the lateral upper structure that you'd normally have if you had a rear seat with a shelf behind it."

> "There is a synergy between the Neon and PT Cruiser. It's not so much that the vehicles are the same or that these vehicles share so many parts. Rather, it's sharing the process, and what we learned on the Neon we were able to apply to the PT Cruiser."
> —Dan Knott

The floor was strengthened by using a transverse beam welded to the floor of the vehicle that connects the two center pillars and ties into the floor pan at the center tunnel. This beam contributes to the side impact protection and increases body stiffness. Because it is placed directly in line with side impact loads, it helps to protect occupants during a side impact collision.

Other side impact forces are distributed through beams located in each door, which direct energy toward the beefy center pillars. Longitudinally, the PT Cruiser is reinforced along the drivetrain tunnel, the body rails, and in the windshield A-pillars. Even the front wheelwells are reinforced to distribute crash forces through the tires and down the sills rather than into the passenger compartment.

Even though the PT Cruiser has short front and rear overhangs, additional steps were taken to ensure that the vehicle meets 5-mile-per-hour impact standards, even though federal requirements call for only 2.5-mile-per-hour protection.

"One of the things we did was push the ends of the body rails all the way out to the face of the bumper beams," said Laginess. "It was absolutely critical for getting maximum impact performance with a very short distance. The structure starts to manage the energy and a front impact is directed behind the fascia. It starts acting very quickly in any kind of event to provide ride down at a good deceleration rate." In other words, it works quickly to dissipate the energy of even the most minor impacts.

In the rear, the principle is the same, but the hardware is different. "We don't have an engine in there," Laginess pointed out, "so we have a little more space to work with and therefore we're able to do the same job with a little less substantial structure than you would use at the front."

Beyond the body structure, there are a whole host of safety features inside the PT Cruiser to protect the passengers in the event of a crash. Of course, seatbelts are the first line of defense in any accident, but the PT Cruiser is unique in that the belts themselves are integrated into the seats, making them easier to use as well as making the seats themselves easier to remove and install. By integrating the belts into the seat, the PT Cruiser also provides the center rear passenger with a three-point belt.

The MacPherson strut front suspension is similar to the one used by Chrysler on the Neon sedan. *Chrysler*

A totally new rear suspension was designed using a twist-beam setup and a Watts linkage. It provides a stable ride and is compact enough to open up the rear cargo space. *Chrysler*

The latest in airbag technology has also been employed. On the driver's side, the airbag works with the steering column, telescoping column coupling, and instrument panel knee bolster to provide additional restraint during collisions. It's hard to believe that there's an airbag in the small, circular hub of the steering wheel, but it's in there. That bag is actually smaller in size and uses a lighter material than previous airbags and yet it meets all federal regulations. The bag is fired by a cleaner-burning propellant,

Dual front airbags are neatly packaged into the small steering wheel hub on the driver's side and behind the body-colored panel on the passenger's side of the dash. *Chrysler*

The optional side airbag, which comes standard when the PT Cruiser is equipped with leather seating, is mounted on the outboard seat rail. The large bag offers both head and chest protection in side impacts. *Chrysler*

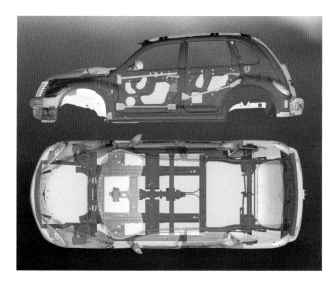

Extensive computer modeling provided the means to develop a body that is structurally sound and yet has the required crumple zones to maximize safety. The PT Cruiser's body is reinforced with cross-body structures that in effect combine the rigidity of a ladder frame with the low cost construction of a unit body. *Chrysler*

A stiff structure is the key to optimizing the performance of all the other components, like the suspension. This cutaway shows how the MacPherson strut front and the twist-beam rear suspensions are attached to the PT Cruiser. In addition to the transverse braces, the vehicle is completely reinforced fore-to-aft with additional stampings welded to the floorpan. *Chrysler*

which eliminates the need for filter screens used on the old airbags to trap the dust from the propellant. The lack of filter screens and the new, lighter bag material eliminate bulk and allow for more compact packaging beneath the steering wheel hub.

One of the reasons the propellant burns cleaner is that the bag employs a hybrid inflator, which uses a small pyrotechnic charge and heat-compressed inert gas stored in a high-pressure cylinder.

Additional crash protection comes from optional side impact airbags that deploy from the sides of the front bucket seats. Using the same hybrid inflator found in the front bags, the side airbags issue from a clamshell case

mounted on an outboard bracket attached to the seat frame. The fully deployed side airbag covers an area of 15 by 26 inches, providing both head and thorax protection.

PT Cruisers are also equipped with an accident-response illumination system that automatically turns on the dome light and unlocks the power door locks when an airbag is deployed.

Special attention has been paid to the headliner and interior hard trim to lessen the effects of head impacts by using softer materials with more "give." Likewise, the seat structures have been specifically designed to absorb impact energy and the seatbelts are equipped with pre-tensioners to take up belt slack in the event of a crash.

The best crash protection is being able to avoid one in the first place. The standard brakes on the PT Cruiser feature front vented discs with single-piston sliding calipers. The rotors are 10.94 inches in diameter for a swept area of 198.5 square inches. At the rear, the PT

While on the European drive, the engineers check out the usefulness of the PT Cruiser's tailgate table feature. *Chrysler*

Cruiser uses drum brakes that are 8.66 inches in diameter and have a swept area of 86 square inches.

Four-wheel disc brakes with ABS are optional. The front discs are similar to those used on the disc/drum setup, while the rears are 10.62-inch solid discs with a swept area of 173.4 inches. The rear discs also use a single-piston sliding caliper.

To protect the PT Cruiser when it's not in use, the optional Sentry Key Theft Deterrent System (standard on European models) uses a chip embedded in the key that talks to a module mounted on the steering column. The steering module will only recognize the frequency emitted from the key chip and won't let the vehicle run without it.

From the advanced electronics of the antitheft system to the ingenious design of the body structure, there's much more to the PT Cruiser than its hip exterior design. It's all these unseen elements that make this vehicle something special in action.

CHAPTER FIVE

CRUISIN' IN THE CRUISER

Driving the PT Cruiser is a bit like being in a Viper or Prowler. Not that the performance is the same, but rather, you find yourself the center of attention.

That's not bad for a vehicle that starts at $16,500 including destination charges.

Early on engineers discovered the magnetism of the styling. Since the PT Cruiser was unveiled more than a year before its on-sale date, the development team had the luxury of performing its final testing and calibration with undisguised prototypes. They were overwhelmed at the reaction that was generated no matter where they went.

"We drove both right- and left-hand-drive PTs in six countries in Europe in the course of a week," said Ernie Laginess, director of body engineering. "I'll never forget being on the autobahn in Germany and being passed up by a family in a big Mercedes. The lady of the family was in the front seat and as the car went by, I could just see her head do a 180. Anytime we stopped, whether it was a rest stop or a gas stop or for the evening at a hotel, we were mobbed. It didn't make any difference if it was France, England, Germany, Switzerland, or Wales—it was always the same.

"We found the same thing here in the U.S., whether we drove the cars locally in Michigan or out West. We went into Red Rock Canyon near Las Vegas and met a couple of Boy Scouts and their leader, and they barraged us with questions for 30 minutes. The vehicle gets an amazing response from people, no matter where you go."

For some, just being seen in the PT Cruiser would be enough. The novelty factor alone will ensure that the PT Cruiser will be a hot product during the first year or so of production. But the Chrysler team understands that the PT Cruiser is more than just a styling exercise. To have real staying power in the market, it has to be a real vehicle. It not only has to look good, it has to have competent driving dynamics and a useful interior. In short, the PT Cruiser has to look great and be functional

From any angle, the PT Cruiser is a blast to drive. *John Lamm*

if it is to survive in a market that offers a myriad of transportation choices.

The PT Cruiser delivers on this score. It starts with something as simple as the body jewelry. The winged Chrysler badges look upscale. The door handles are chromed with substantial pushbuttons to release the latches. The rear decklid has a large Chrysler badge that doubles as a hatch release. A quick glance inside base models reveals standard air conditioning, tilt steering, six-speaker AM/FM stereo with cassette, intermittent wipers, and tinted glass. Inside, you'll also find four cupholders, a washable pop-out coin holder, large map pockets, and a flexible storage bin with a moveable tray.

Uplevel PT Cruiser Limited Edition models add features from three packages, the Light Group, Luxury Touring Group, and Moonroof Group, which are optional on base models. Limited Edition versions come with sliding sun visors with illuminated vanity mirrors, reading lamps integrated into the rearview mirror, two auxiliary power points (one in the center stack and one in the cargo area), and a console-mounted flood lamp.

At first touch, the PT Cruiser feels substantial thanks to details such as chromed door handles with push-button releases. *John Lamm*

From the Luxury Touring Group, Limited Edition models receive fog lamps, chrome exhaust tips, touring tuned suspension, leather-wrapped steering wheel and shift knob (on automatic versions), 16-inch chromed aluminum wheels, and floor mats embroidered with the PT Cruiser logo. Finally, the Limited Edition also sports a power moonroof with a one-touch-open switch and sliding sunshade, and an overhead console with compass and temperature display.

The Limited Edition comes so well equipped that there are only a handful of options, including four-wheel disc brakes, traction control and ABS, an upgraded sound system with CD player, an engine block heater, and a roof rack with two continuously adjustable cross bars and quick-release latches.

There's also a wide selection of colors, starting with the Aztek Yellow (the same gold hue of the Pronto Cruizer concept cars), Silver Metallic, Black, Inferno Red, Patriot Blue, Aquamarine Metallic, Taupe Frost Metallic, Stone White, Deep Cranberry, and Shale Green Metallic.

Beneath the bright colors and sexy sheet metal is a real car—or for government purposes, a truck. Although the PT Cruiser is based heavily on car components, its unique flat floor qualifies it as a truck under EPA rules. While the PT Cruiser does meet car fuel economy, safety, and emission standards, the fact that it is considered a truck helps the company's overall truck numbers when it comes to meeting Corporate Average Fuel Economy standards.

That flat load floor helps deliver nearly the same interior space as a short-wheelbase minivan. As a result, when you're seated inside the PT Cruiser, the surroundings feel familiar. The upright seating position gives you the impression of sitting in a much larger vehicle. The combination of this high H-point and the forward rake of the body provides excellent visibility. Engineers were able to maximize outward visibility and spaciousness by using virtual reality technology in placing the A-pillars. The front buckets are supportive and manually adjustable for rake.

The cabin is spacious and logically laid out. The center console houses a cup holder and storage bin. Note the leather-covered shifter on the automatic. *John Lamm*

The cowl isn't particularly low, but it's not in the way either. The dashboard, like that in the minivan, doesn't protrude very far from the firewall. This positioning of the instrument panel does much to add to the feeling of spaciousness in the forward cabin. There's plenty of elbow-room between the front bucket seats, and, despite the PT Cruiser's fairly narrow nose, you don't feel hemmed in.

The retro feel that interior designers wanted comes through loud and clear with the body-colored inserts on both sides of the dash. The passenger-side insert hides an airbag, while the driver's side is divided into three circles for the instruments. Even though the instruments are recessed a fair amount, they are easily read, thanks to the white faces with Art Deco–inspired graphics. Another neat touch is the four-spoke steering wheel with a hub so small you think that there's no way they packaged an airbag in it (but they assure us there's one in there). The wheel has a nice grippy feel and spokes placed at nine and three o'clock provide a nice resting place for your thumbs.

The center stack houses round, louvered vents that look like they came from a 1950s-era air conditioner, while the sound system and heating, ventilation, and air-conditioning controls are a few of the modern touches with fairly conventional controls. These switches and buttons are straightforward in their presentation and easy to operate.

The driver's front bucket has a center fold-down armrest (the passenger doesn't get one), and the center console–mounted shifter for the manual has a chrome shaft and Bakelite-inspired ball on the end of it. Automatics settle for a modern shift lever trimmed in leather. The console itself has open bins that act as cup holders, and there's a larger open storage area that runs the length of the console, which is flanked by the hand brake. Don't look on the doors for the standard power window lifts; the front-door switches are located on the dash between the vents, while the rear-door switches are placed at the back of the center console, ostensibly to make them accessible to both front and rear passengers.

After the start of production, the PT Cruiser will get additional storage in an underseat storage drawer located beneath the passenger-side front bucket.

The powertrain on the PT Cruiser is good, but not great. The 2.4-liter dohc four-cylinder engine, which provides 150 brake horsepower at 5,600 rpm and 162 ft-lb of torque at 4,000 rpm, operates smoothly and efficiently, thanks in part to balance shaft technology. For the most part, it's fairly quiet, with a bit of induction snarl and exhaust snort on full-throttle acceleration.

The engine, when equipped with the five-speed manual gearbox, allows the PT Cruiser to scoot to 60 miles per hour in about nine seconds, which is fairly respectable for a vehicle weighing 3,200 pounds.

The five-speed manual makes the PT Cruiser as fun to drive as it is to look at. Even though it has a cable linkage and a fairly long shifter, the throws are short

Controls for the front windows are positioned in the center of the dash so that both driver and passenger have easy access. The rear window switches are located on the back of the center console so all passengers can operate them. *John Lamm*

The doors feature integral map pockets; the pulls are configured to match the contour of the human hand and the releases, like the outside handles, are chromed. *John Lamm*

The manual-equipped PT Cruiser features a shifter with a round knob that simulates vintage Bakelite. The ball sits atop a chromed lever. *John Lamm*

and precise. There's no vagueness, and the clutch takeup is light and easily modulated. The retro ball atop the shifter fits snugly in the palm of your hand, adding to the delightful feel of the manual.

Expect slower times for models equipped with the four-speed automatic transmission. That gearbox, though

it does sap some of the life from the engine, provides smooth, solid shifts. The adaptive logic in the electronic controller does a good job providing crisp, timely upshifts while preventing the engine from hunting back and forth between the top two gears.

The other factor to keep in mind is that acceleration tests have been performed with only the presence of a driver. Load the PT Cruiser with two adults and three children and maybe some luggage, and the limitations of the 2.4-liter four will begin to be a factor. While the styling screams out small-block V-8, there's no way a six, much less an eight, can be packaged in the coffin-style nose. But turbocharged versions of the PT Cruiser are not out of the question.

Though the engine could use a little more muscle, it is efficient. The EPA fuel economy ratings are 20 miles per gallon city/26 miles per gallon highway, and with a 15-gallon fuel tank, range is estimated at just a tick under 300 miles.

The suspension, which features independent front MacPherson struts and a rear twist-beam with coil springs and Watts linkage, is sprung more for carrying people and stuff rather than apex carving. With its wheels pushed all the way out to the corners, the PT Cruiser provides a comfortable ride while exhibiting a slight tendency toward understeer, which is a trait associated with most front-drive vehicles.

The handling overall is generally predictable, although the combination of upright seating and tall body gives a perception of more body lean than the suspension will allow. When pushed hard on the slalom and skidpad, the PT Cruiser demonstrates that it has much greater grip than the body motions would have you believe. But mainly, the PT Cruiser is a competent-handling car that won't punish you with a too-stiff suspension (though from the hot rod looks, you might

With all the seats, including the front passenger bucket, folded down, the PT Cruiser can haul an 8-foot ladder with the liftgate closed. *John Lamm*

expect a real kidney-pounding ride). Actually the ride of the PT Cruiser is quite benign, which may come as a surprise to people used to small vehicles that hop and dart across road irregularities.

Complementing this user-friendly suspension is the power-assisted steering. The action is direct and precise without feeling overboosted and yet it has enough assist to make even the tightest parking maneuvers a snap.

The turning radius curb-to-curb on manual versions with the base tire is 36.5 feet, while automatic models with 16-inch tires make the turn in 39.7 feet.

While the standard disc/drum brakes have enough stopping power for the vehicle, the feel and control of the optional four-wheel disc package is superior. And with four-wheel discs come ABS and traction control, two items that alone are worth the price of the upgrade.

A movable shelf located behind the second seat can be adjusted to five different positions, including this one as a picnic table for tailgate parties. *John Lamm*

Along with the better brakes, another option worth considering is the larger wheel and tire package. The PT Cruiser comes with steel disc 15-inch wheels shod with P195/65R-15 Goodyear Eagle LS all-season touring tires as standard equipment. The optional package includes 16-inch aluminum wheels with P205/55R-16 Goodyear LS all-season rubber.

European models are equipped with the 15-inch steel wheels with P195/65HR-15 Goodyear NCT5 tires, while the optional 16-inch alloy wheels get P205/55HR-16 Goodyear NCT5 performance tires. Europeans can also opt for P185/65HR-15 Goodyear Eagle Vector performance tires on the 15-inch rims.

Even though the PT Cruiser is basically a big box on wheels, the body is surprisingly stiff. Wind noise, vibration, and harshness are nicely damped, though you will notice a bit of engine buzz that manages to work its way back into the cabin. Fit and finish, as well as the use of materials, is top notch for a vehicle with a base price of $16,500.

While the PT Cruiser's style definitely stands out in the crowd and its performance can run with the pack, its real ace-in-the-hole is the flexible interior. It truly allows you to tailor the PT Cruiser to your own needs, even on a whim. If the styling says you've got to have it, the PT Cruiser's utility provides all the rationale you need to justify the purchase.

The rear seats, thanks to the stepped theater-style mounting, offer excellent visibility out of the vehicle without compromising headroom. Legroom is also pretty good; the trick here is the upright seating. Since the rear passengers sit higher, their legs are more upright, which adds to the impression of spaciousness. Access to the rear seating compartment is also made easier with doors that open as wide as 74 degrees, nearly 10 degrees more than conventional sedans. Rear-passenger comfort is also enhanced with ducts built into the floor that direct heated air to the feet.

The clincher is the number of ways the front-passenger bucket and the rear seats can be folded, flipped,

The seats can be folded flat and easily removed from the vehicle. Small wheels on the base help to move them around. *John Lamm*

or removed altogether in order to make the most of the cavernous cargo hold. According to Chrysler, there are up to 26 different configurations for the interior.

The rear bench is actually two seats, split 65/35. Each side can be independently flipped forward, folded and tumbled forward, or removed to provide additional room for cargo. The passenger bucket's seatback can be folded flat forward providing a workspace or even a lunch table for the driver. As a result of this flexibility, the PT Cruiser can carry one, two, three, four, or five passengers (including driver), depending on configuration. The removable rear seats feature integrated seatbelts, which makes removal and installation a snap. The center seating position also has a three-point belt, and the latches that hold the seatback in the upright position also support the shoulder belt loads on the outboard passengers. Tie down loops for child-seat tethers mount on the seatback behind each seating position. The removable back seats also include a carrying handle and small rollers to ease moving and storage. Seat removal requires no tools.

With both rear seats removed, the flat cargo hold can accommodate a variety of large or long objects—up to 64 cubic feet worth. That load space is a full 3.5 feet between the wheelwells and 5 feet long at the floor. The liftgate opens 33.5 inches high, 39.9 inches wide, and the liftover from the ground is only 24.9 inches. Both the rear seats and passenger-side front bucket fold flat at the same level, enabling the PT Cruiser to carry objects as long as 8 feet with the rear liftgate closed.

Although cargo space behind the back seat is somewhat limited—19 cubic feet with the rear seat in place—the most is made of that space thanks to an innovative removable shelf.

"The idea of the rear shelf panel came from a discussion we had with one of the suppliers," said Tom Edson, director of interior systems engineering. "They hired a guy who was driving around in a minivan with privacy glass and a video camera. This guy drove down the highway and did the 'Candid Camera' thing with people and how they use their cars.

"One of the observations he made is that at a rest stop everyone has all the doors open and the liftgate up and they're moving things around. The space of the car actually extends beyond the sheet metal. We thought about that and then came up with the idea for the rear shelf. We'd

THE SHAPE.

The overall shape of the PT Cruiser is tough, yet huggable. The vehicle's tough-guy looks come from a wide stance underscored by flared fenders and a body inset from the wheels. Gray colored front and rear bumpers also add strong truck-like cues to the overall design. Along the rockers, flaring of the sills catches the light and breaks up the body. In addition to recalling running boards, the detailing along the lower edge of the vehicle keeps the vehicle from appearing slab-sided. While still looking substantial, the blacked-out B- and C-pillars reduce the mass of the greenhouse thereby accentuating the muscularity of the lower half of the vehicle. The forward gesture of the design comes from an aggressive slant to the hatchback. The D-pillar has an abrupt breakover into a roof that also slants forward, giving the PT Cruiser an almost "chopped top" appearance. In addition to the grille giving the car a retro look, the cutline for the engine bay gives the appearance of the hood resting on top of the body. That line continues down the entire side of the vehicle as a character line, neatly bisected by the cutlines for the doors. *John Lamm*

This sequence shows just a few of the 26 different configurations the flip-and-fold seats afford in the PT Cruiser. It starts with just one side of the 65/35 rear seat folded down, then both sides down, followed by one side flipped up, and then both sides folded and flipped. Finally, you can take the rear seats out altogether to maximize cargo room. *John Lamm*

seen package trays that did different things. Some would tip up, some actually move in a number of different places. We thought 'Why not increase the interior space beyond the door openings?'" Edson explained. "We were thinking of the oven concept, where you pull your oven rack out and it extends beyond the door of the oven. So we thought, 'Why not do something like that with the rear shelf?' That's where we got the idea of the tailgate party position."

And from that a number of positions for the rear shelf, which also provides a measure of security for the cargo hold, were devised. In all, Edson developed five different configurations. In the top position, the shelf is level with the upright rear seat backs to protect the entire cargo area. In the mid-position, the shelf is level with the rear seats when the backs are folded forward. This provides a smaller secure area beneath the shelf panel. The shelf can also be locked on the floor either upright or flipped over to reveal its utility side, a rubberized surface that provides a washable surface

> "I'll never forget being on the autobahn in Germany and being passed up by a family in a big Mercedes. The lady of the family was in the front seat and as the car went by, I could just see her head do a 180. Anytime we stopped, whether it was a rest stop or a gas stop or for the evening at a hotel, we were mobbed. It didn't make any difference if it was France, England, Germany, Switzerland, or Wales—it was always the same."
> —*Ernie Laginess*

to carry dirty items such as gardening equipment and supplies. The shelf can also be tipped sideways in a vertical position to divide the passenger and cargo compartments. Hooks on the utility side of the panel can be used to secure grocery bags. Finally, the shelf has a tailgate position, which allows it to extend outside over the rear bumper held in place by a fold-out support.

The shelf even has notched corners as part of a feature to prevent children from being trapped in the rear compartment. The notches are big enough for small hands to reach through and trip the buttons that release the back seats.

"When we took our drive in Europe, we were constantly on the move. We had our box lunches and that picnic tray really works. It really is convenient," Edson reported. "I've demonstrated the seats and rear shelf unit a dozen times and people can't resist visualizing themselves using this vehicle. That's the kind of thing we wanted to achieve here."

CHAPTER SIX

BUILDING THEM SOUTH OF THE BORDER

It's no coincidence that two of the hottest cars to hit the market in recent years, the PT Cruiser and Volkswagen's New Beetle, are both built in the same country—Mexico.

The PT Cruiser is assembled at DaimlerChrysler's Toluca plant, while the New Beetle is built in Puebla, about 100 miles away.

The easy answer to why would be wages; but actually the answer is more complicated than that. Certainly, the North America Free Trade Agreement (NAFTA), which opened up the borders along the United States, Canada, and Mexico, has played a major role in the decision. Exchange and labor rates are favorable, and by boosting production within Mexico, both DaimlerChrysler and Volkswagen earn valuable credits toward importing vehicles not produced in that country for sale there.

Even more important are the assembly plants themselves. Both Toluca and Puebla are midsize plants capable of producing 150,000 to 180,000 units annually, as opposed to the behemoth plants in the United States and Germany that are geared toward making upwards of 250,000 units each year.

Like the decision-makers for the New Beetle, Chrysler execs were conservative in their estimates of PT Cruiser demand, aiming, like VW, at selling a maximum of 180,000 units a year worldwide. Both companies knew that there would be a heavy initial demand for these breakthrough vehicles. The question that weighs heavily is for how long? Over time, both companies have learned the hard way that it is often better to build a few less than a few too many.

So DaimlerChrysler settled on its Toluca plant, which is located about 35 miles southwest of Mexico City. Toluca is an industrial town of about 2 million people and is also home to some General Motors factories as well as other nonautomotive businesses such as pharmaceuticals. Over the years, the Toluca plant has produced primarily passenger cars and trucks for

Team leaders on the assembly line received training in Michigan where they worked alongside the engineers who designed the PT Cruiser's components. *Chrysler*

The sprawling Toluca, Mexico, assembly plant, which builds the PT Cruiser, is located only about 100 miles from VW's Puebla factory, which builds the New Beetle. *Chrysler*

the Mexican market. In the post-NAFTA era, there has been a transition to building vehicles for all markets. The most notable has been the Chrysler Sebring convertible, for which the plant was the sole worldwide source.

"The workforce is very talented, very skilled," said Scott Wilkins, program manager for the PT Cruiser. "They have demonstrated the ability to build as many as five different models at the same time and do them with a high level of quality."

Wilkins said the most important element in assigning PT Cruiser production was finding a plant with the capacity to build a niche vehicle. "The Toluca assembly plant did that and did an excellent job of building 50,000 to 60,000 Sebring convertibles per year. So if you are looking for a plant to build upwards of 60,000 vehicles per year, Toluca would be your first choice as opposed to a plant that has traditionally done high-volume products. We based the decision more on their ability to be versatile in terms of building a number of different units at high quality than its location or labor cost or anything else. It isn't the low-cost solution by any means."

The plant's established track record of building Sebring convertibles, as well as products as diverse as the Neon coupe, Dodge Stratus sedan, and Dodge Ramcharger, meant the plant was well equipped to take on an all-new vehicle such as the PT Cruiser. But first room had to be made at the plant. Coincidentally, the Sebring convertible, as well as the Chrysler Cirrus sedan (which would be renamed the Sebring sedan) and the Dodge Stratus were all slated for makeovers. Sebring convertible production would be shifted to the company's Sterling Heights, Michigan, assembly plant, where they would be built alongside the sedans. However, the plant would be winding down Sebring convertible production as it was revving up the PT Cruiser build.

"Bringing a brand-new vehicle in an all-new segment like the PT Cruiser to market quickly—from concept to volume production—is always an enormous task," said Gary Henson, DaimlerChrysler Executive Vice President of Manufacturing. "Although the launch curve was ambitious, we maintained our schedule and shipped product. We didn't lose any production and we stayed focused on quality throughout the entire process."

That focus enabled the company to keep total PT Cruiser startup costs below $600 million, a remarkable feat in an era where redesigning an existing model can cost more than $1 billion.

"Bringing the PT Cruiser to market quickly for relatively low cost is the result of taking advantage of new technologies in development, implementing best practices throughout the launch, and cutting waste to produce repeatable, reliable, world-class quality. The goal is to get better with every launch and we're doing that," Henson said.

A big part of that story actually begins in Auburn Hills, Michigan, at the company's technical center, where advance work upstream means a smoother launch and a higher-quality build at the plant in Mexico. Ernie Laginess, director of body engineering for the small-car platform, said that advanced computer modeling allows engineers to produce a virtual-reality build of the PT Cruiser even before the first body panel has been stamped.

"One of the things we used extensively is our total quality control system for body dimension," he said. "We started out early using a program called variation simulation analysis. Once we set the dimensional requirements of the vehicle, we can essentially take the design and how all the parts are going to fit together—we call that shingling—and what each tolerance on each part is, and feed it into a large computer program. We build a thousand hypothetical vehicles and see what the distribution of the dimensional variations is on every part of the car.

"So after you've built all these vehicles, you can see the distribution of the tolerance—how many are built with nominal variation and how many are built with a half-millimeter over or under tolerance."

In essence, Laginess' group built a model to predict what would happen when actual PT Cruisers would be built. This information is crucial in setting up the final dimensions and tolerances for the production vehicle.

> "Bringing the PT Cruiser to market quickly for relatively low cost is the result of taking advantage of new technologies in development, implementing best practices throughout the launch, and cutting waste to produce repeatable, reliable, world-class quality." —Gary Henson

Sheet steel is fed into presses by robots. Body panels are stamped and mash welded, a process that is able to bond metal of different thicknesses. *Chrysler*

"We built a library of past practices and by having this computer program, we can try different alternatives for how we shingle the car, what kind of tolerances we can demand, and even how we set up the assembly sequence. We can see which one gives us the optimum build in terms of dimensional integrity," Laginess said.

Five months ahead of the launch date, the C-1 [or first] build of pilot vehicles began. As a result of the computer modeling, these prototype vehicles were actually being built at levels that were better than the launch target.

"The goal was to launch this car at a dimensional integrity that is higher than the old vehicle [Sebring convertible] that it replaces in the plant," Laginess said. "We did that at the start of production. We were meeting that prior to launch and are continuing to make progress. It's great to have a dimensionally correct body because you're going to get superior fits, and people are going to notice that the doors fit and they operate great. The liftgate, the hood, everything has a high-quality look to it."

All this from a $16,000 vehicle.

But the benefits of a tight-fitting body don't stop there. If all the master dimensions are correct, then all the mechanical parts—from the drivetrain to the suspension pieces that attach to the body—also work better with less noise, vibration, and harshness.

"The body is the foundation everything else hangs on," Laginess said. "If everything on the vehicle comes together in an optimal way, it pays huge dividends for us."

The remarkable thing is that all this has come together with a plant that is more than 2,500 miles from the technical center. Laginess said a special computer program was written for dimensional templates specifically for use on the Sebring convertible as it went into production at Toluca. It was the first such software application and it was expanded when the Neon coupe was added at that plant. The latest update for the PT Cruiser is now online, allowing information to flow on a daily basis back

As a PT Cruiser is moved down the assembly line, note the body protection that is employed to protect the paint finish from accidental scratches or blemishes. *Chrysler*

Workers hoist the engine and transaxle into the PT Cruiser from below. By raising the body on an overhead carrier, it makes the job of mating the drivetrain to the car easier. *Chrysler*

and forth between the technical center and the plant. As that data is collected at the plant, it can be accessed by engineers in Detroit, at the plant, or anywhere along the supplier chain.

Currently, the Toluca plant has the capacity to build 40 vehicles per hour. As PT Cruiser production ramped up, the number of Dodge Stratus sedans and Sebring convertibles was slowly decreased as production

Following a dip in primer, this PT Cruiser body is headed toward the paint shop. *Chrysler*

of the new versions of the latter two grew in Michigan. At full production, Toluca is capable of building 180,000 PT Cruisers annually using 3,400 workers on two shifts.

Those workers received extensive training, with teams involved early in the design engineering verification process. Team members from Mexico were sent to Auburn Hills, where they actually built prototype vehicles

As production of the PT Cruiser ramps up, production of the Sebring convertible, which is built on the same line, begins to taper off. By the time the PT Cruiser reaches full-line rate, Sebring convertible production will have been moved to Sterling Heights, Michigan. *Chrysler*

at a special pilot plant that allowed them to work alongside the engineers who designed the components. These teams were comprised of core production workers representing every workstation at the Toluca plant. They spent six weeks each at the pilot plant over an eight-month period. These workers in turn trained fellow team members back at the plant. Ultimately, one team member per workstation was trained in Auburn Hills, which was

A combination of men and machines builds the PT Cruiser in Toluca, Mexico. *Chrysler*

approximately one in every four workers at the Toluca plant. Each trainer received more than 500 hours of training.

Following the pilot build in Michigan, preproduction vehicles were built right on the assembly line during normal production, which helped refine the build process and ensure repeatability and standardization of procedures. Running preproduction vehicles through

The symmetrical design of the
instrument panel allows for a
cost-effective conversion of
the PT Cruiser to right-hand
drive for such key markets as
Japan, Great Britain, and
Australia. *Chrysler*

the plant in this way also shortened development time and lowered launch costs, another factor enabling the PT Cruiser to have a low sticker price.

In addition to the computer model that predicted build quality going in, the Toluca plant has an ongoing program of monitoring dimensional accuracy. Eight full bodies per day are measured using 2,000 different points of reference. Individual workstations are responsible for quality and any problems spotted on the line are addressed immediately. Audits are taken daily of welds and seals, body and paint, and final assembly. All vehicle electrical and mechanical systems are tested, and each vehicle undergoes a water and road test before being shipped.

Vehicles are assembled using the latest practices in just-in-time deliveries. The plant maintains about a day and a half of parts inventories, which further reduces cost and waste. A number of parts suppliers have located near the plant to better serve the assembly process. Along these lines, an on-site satellite stamping plant provides body panels. The PT Cruiser is also the first product in the DaimlerChrysler system to use "mash welding," which allows different thicknesses of steel to be joined, resulting in better fits and higher quality.

Initially, the PT Cruiser production at Toluca included both right- and left-hand-drive models with 2.0- and 2.4-liter versions for the world market. In April 2000, the first shipment of 450 PT Cruisers left Toluca for Veracruz, where the vehicles were loaded on transports for the three-week trip to Europe.

Four shipments per week were scheduled with total export volume of about 18,000 units to Europe and 5,000 units to the rest of the world.

Due to higher-than-anticipated demand in both America and Europe, company officials decided shortly after the PT Cruiser's launch to add a second production site, this one in Europe. DaimlerChrysler chose its Eurostar plant in Graz, Austria, which builds Chrysler Voyager minivans and Jeep Grand Cherokees for Europe.

"Eurostar has the capacity, track record, and location to best support Europe and the rest-of-the-world markets with PT Cruisers," Henson said of the announced expansion. Eventually, all 2.0-liter and right-hand-drive models will be built alongside left-hand-drive export models at Eurostar—some 50,000 units per year. This will allow Toluca to concentrate only on left-hand-drive 2.4-liter units for the North American market. If initial demand is any indication, Chrysler will need every one of them.

CHAPTER SEVEN

THE CRUISE CONTINUES

Prior to March 2000, the PT Cruiser's official on-sale date, Chrysler received more than 300,000 inquiries from potential customers. Of course, officially unveiling the car more than a year before it was sold gave Chrysler a unique opportunity to promote this product.

During that 14-month interval, Chrysler communicated with those prospects through e-mail and direct-mail campaigns that included sending what amounted to mini-press kits with full specifications. These prospects also received informational videos and invitations to test-drive the PT Cruiser at a local dealer.

A promotion was even devised around the unique tailgate table. Called the PT Cruiser Tailgate Party, the program took prototypes to 10 college football games where up to 375,000 people had the opportunity to see the car.

According to Jay Kuhnie, director of Chrysler communications, "The emotional draw of the PT Cruiser gave us the unique opportunity to build a relationship with people before the first one even went on sale."

This translated into an instant sell-out. Dealers ordered all 130,000 of the first year's production resulting in waiting lists, and in some instances, premiums of $2,500 to $4,000 over sticker being charged. Even Chrysler was quick to cash in, raising the $16,000 base price 4 percent to $16,500 within a month of the vehicle's launch.

With an eventual maximum capacity of 180,000 in Mexico, plus 50,000 or so in Europe, company officials are wrestling with the possibility of adding yet another plant.

The first impulse is to try to meet this overwhelming demand. On the other hand, as Chrysler learned with the Viper, Mazda with the Miata, and Volkswagen with the New Beetle, initial demand of a breakthrough product shouldn't be confused with staying power. Once this initial surge is over, the challenge lies in keeping the PT Cruiser concept fresh in order to attract new buyers.

Of course, that need to freshen the product can be put off as long as sales remain robust. It was nearly two

The GT Cruiser, a customized version of the PT Cruiser, was introduced at a parts aftermarket trade show in Las Vegas in late 1999. Beneath the hood is a turbocharged version of the 2.4-liter four that makes 200 horsepower. *Chrysler*

Adding to the custom feel of the GT Cruiser is the fact that it's lowered about an inch with the use of new suspension bits. The rear hatch has a cleaner look with the badge/liftgate release repositioned at the bottom of the hatch. *Chrysler*

years after the launch of the New Beetle that Volkswagen introduced its first major change—the more powerful Turbo model—to give sales a boost. A convertible version would wait until four years after launch for its debut.

Still, even before the PT Cruiser went on sale, designers and engineers were busy working on future iterations. In keeping with the idea that the PT Cruiser was developed in plain sight, they didn't keep their ideas secret.

At the 1999 Specialty Equipment Market Association (SEMA) show in Las Vegas, Chrysler took the wraps off the GT Cruiser, a customized PT that fit in well with this show, which is geared to the huge parts and accessories aftermarket.

The GT Cruiser was designed to underscore the vehicle's appeal to the youth market as well as those seeking a vehicle that is easily adapted to suit individual tastes.

"The PT Cruiser already is difficult to categorize," Tom Gale said at the GT Cruiser unveiling. "With the GT Cruiser, we're showing the SEMA show participants—who are all about customizing and tuning—how one could take the PT Cruiser to the next level: lowered, with subtle design modifications and added power."

The GT Cruiser recognizes that there is a substantial segment of PT buyers who will not be satisfied with a stock vehicle. It's one way of showing that the PT Cruiser is almost a blank canvas that is just waiting to be customized.

"A PT Cruiser can be whatever the individual owner wants it to be. It fits any lifestyle. Some may see it as a tribute to the classic era, some as a street rod, others as a multifaceted and functional light truck in a class of its own. There's really nothing like it on the road today." —*Tom Gale*

A sketch of the GT Cruiser shows a much more extreme machine, with a high wing and a wider-open and more aggressive grille. *Chrysler*

The GT Cruiser is equipped with a turbocharged engine that boosts output as high as 225 horsepower. *Chrysler*

Lower and sleeker than the stock vehicle, the GT Cruiser gets its go-fast looks by following traditional customizing guidelines, according to Kenneth Carlson, senior designer in charge of the GT Cruiser. "However, we applied a distinct modern design vocabulary to the modifications. By lowering the vehicle by 1 inch and by widening the track by 2 inches, we gave it a mildly 'slammed' impression. We also removed the badges from the hood and deck and integrated the bumpers into the fascia. On the GT Cruiser, the badges are incorporated in the grille and rear license plate brow, as you would see on a classic hot rod."

The GT Cruiser presents a totally different face due to a bumper that was integrated behind the front fascia. The main grille has been shortened considerably and a secondary grille with an aggressive opening was added below the bumper line. Two huge driving lights flank this more pronounced lower grille, which gives the GT Cruiser a powerful look.

Although the company has no immediate plans to build it, the Panel Cruiser caused quite a stir at the 2000 North American International Auto Show. *Chrysler*

The wheelwells have much larger flares to accommodate the bigger 17-inch five-spoke alloy wheels shod with P215/50R-17 tires. On the rear of the vehicle, the badge with integrated latch was moved to the bottom of the hatch to give the rear end a cleaner look. An integrated body-colored rear bumper also enhanced the streamlined look, as did the dual chrome exhaust tips, which also underscored the sporty nature of the GT Cruiser.

But the look is far from being merely cosmetic. Beneath the hood, the 2.4-liter four was outfitted with a turbocharger, boosting output by a third to 200 horsepower. Torque was also increased to around 225 ft-lb. In keeping with the higher output of the engine, the transmission was also upgraded. The beefier five-speed manual gearbox comes from the Neon ACR (American Club Racing) parts bin.

In addition to tweaking the output of the engine, the chassis also received some major modifications, which contributed to the lower ride height and wider track. These components included Koni/Mopar MacPherson struts and stiffer sway bars, which also came out of the ACR catalog.

The interior of the Panel Cruiser is functional, yet elegant. The ash-colored wood features chrome skid strips, while the walls have integrated tie-downs to secure all types of cargo. *Chrysler*

The one area that didn't need updating was the interior, which remained stock. Still, the overall GT Cruiser package is just a hint of what the aftermarket is prepared to offer in the way of PT Cruiser upgrades. Gale said, "The distinct personality of the Chrysler PT Cruiser is unmatched by any vehicle on the road. The GT Cruiser show truck also borrows design cues from classic American automobiles, but shows how this design can be individualized to suit anyone's taste."

The second variation on the PT Cruiser theme was unveiled at the 2000 North American International Auto Show. Called the Panel Cruiser, it was yet another concept that appeared before the PT Cruiser had gone on sale.

The two-door panel van was the purest expression yet of the sedan delivery theme that was part of the inspiration for the PT Cruiser.

"We set out to design a more cargo van–like vehicle based on the PT Cruiser, utilizing its abundant interior

Tom Gale (left) and Freeman Thomas (right), one of the New Beetle's designers, discuss the features of the Panel Cruiser at a Southern California cruise night. The Panel Cruiser looks right at home next to the blown 1932 Ford roadster. *John Lamm*

space while maintaining its clean, contemporary lines and youthful appearance," Carlson noted at the vehicle's unveiling. "By replacing the rear doors and windows with panels and the rear seats with a wood floor, we've created a versatile rear cargo space that could be used as a light delivery truck or an individual lifestyle vehicle . . . the possibilities are endless."

While retaining the front bucket seats, the Panel Cruiser was finished with a full wood floor that fea-

tured chrome skid strips and wood bars along the side quarter panels with cargo straps providing a multiuse cargo area.

"We designed the interior to emphasize the volume available in the PT Cruiser," said Jeff Godshall, senior design manager. "By creating a simple rear cargo space with features similar to those found in moving vans, such as wood floors and cargo straps, we invite a multitude of imaginative uses by the owner."

107

The Panel Cruiser shares the same design cues as the GT Cruiser. It stands 1 inch lower and rides on a 2-inch-wider track, thanks to the use of the ACR Koni/Mopar struts and sway bars. Like the GT Cruiser, the Panel Cruiser has larger flared fenders front and rear to house the 17-inch chromed wheels with P215/45R-17 tires.

The front of the Panel Cruiser sports a look similar to the GT Cruiser. Both the front and rear bumpers are hidden beneath the fascias, while the smaller main grille is augmented by the lower intake flanked with

Former DaimlerChrysler chairman Bob Eaton introduces the PT Cruiser and two show versions, the GT Cruiser and Panel Cruiser, using his version of smoke and mirrors. *Chrysler*

To announce the launch of this breakthrough vehicle, a large wallscape was painted on the side of DaimlerChrysler's Auburn Hills, Michigan, headquarters, showing the PT Cruiser crashing through the glass. *Chrysler*

THE CRUISER QUANDRY: HOT ROD OR NOT?
A Hot Rod Designer's Take on the PT Cruiser
By Thom Taylor

Hot rodding customs dictate that cars manufactured after 1948 are not hot rod material; as a result, cars newer than 1948 cannot participate in the hundreds of rodding activities held throughout the United States every year. Therefore, I find it especially interesting and exciting that since May 2000, numerous PT Cruisers have been conspicuously appearing at hot rod functions. Additionally, a multitude of PTs can be seen on the 2000 *Hot Rod Magazine* Power Tour. What's going on?

In 1948, Detroit manufacturers (with a few exceptions) stopped producing cars with separate, protruding fenders and running boards. This epochal (to rodders, anyway) styling event led to the establishment of what is and what isn't hot rod–worthy. However, every rodder I have talked to thinks the PT Cruiser is so cool, which leads to this quandary of the Cruiser: Is it a hot rod, or isn't it?

For more than a year now there has been a buzz about the Cruiser within the hot rod ranks. Many professional rod builders have been anxious to get their hands on a PT to showcase to their customers. These are the cars I've noticed at the rod runs I have recently attended. Additionally, individual rodders have been making plans to buy one "for their wife." (This is hot rod slang for, "I want one real bad but since I have five other hot rods in the garage I'll say it's for my wife so this one doesn't count as the sixth.")

We're not just talking about stock Cruisers with flames and cool wheels. The ones I've seen are lowered with, in some cases, elaborate paint jobs, aftermarket "cat-back" exhausts, and modified grilles. I've even seen a conversion to a folding, canvas-like moon roof similar to "rag top" Volkswagens of the 1950s and 1960s. And this was

The hot rod aftermarket was quick to see the PT Cruiser's potential, and after production was announced it wasn't long before Thom Taylor was penning concept sketches for a number of clients. Hot rodders are often willing to sacrifice practicality for style, hence this rendering of a potential PT Phaeton. Not a vehicle that you'd want to take cross-country, but it would be an ideal beach cruiser.

all within a few weeks of the Cruiser's introduction!

Part of the attraction has to be the PT's similarity to mid-1930s Ford and Chevy sedans. The familiar shapes so dear to the rodding ranks are all present—but there's something else. That something is hard to define, especially when you consider the cool reception hot rodders gave the other Chrysler product that was intended in every way to be a hot rod: the Plymouth Prowler. I heard many a rodder label the Prowler contemptuous, and they grumbled at how Chrysler presumed to think that it could actually create a hot rod, when it had been Detroit's duty for 80 years merely to provide hot rod fodder. Although Plymouth's roadster has gotten better, rodders still turn up their noses at the Prowler.

So it is even more curious that in the Cruiser we have a vehicle that makes no presumptions about being anything, yet has been embraced wholeheartedly by the hard-nosed hot rodders. Maybe that makes for the best product in the end—a vehicle that has the ability to be many things to many people without making airs, along with the versatility to be transformed with simply a little imagination, for those seeking individuality. Whatever the case, to hot rodders throughout the country, the PT Cruiser is the first new car in more than 50 years that has caught their imagination—and their hearts.

The surf-wagon comparison is irresistible when it comes to the PT . . . and what better way to haul your 'boards than with a PT Woodie. Although it's simple to do, it should be done right with real wood veneer, not vinyl.

The Panel Cruiser concept is the ideal advertising vehicle . . . especially when it's built for a hot rod aftermarket company and decked out in a flamed paint job.

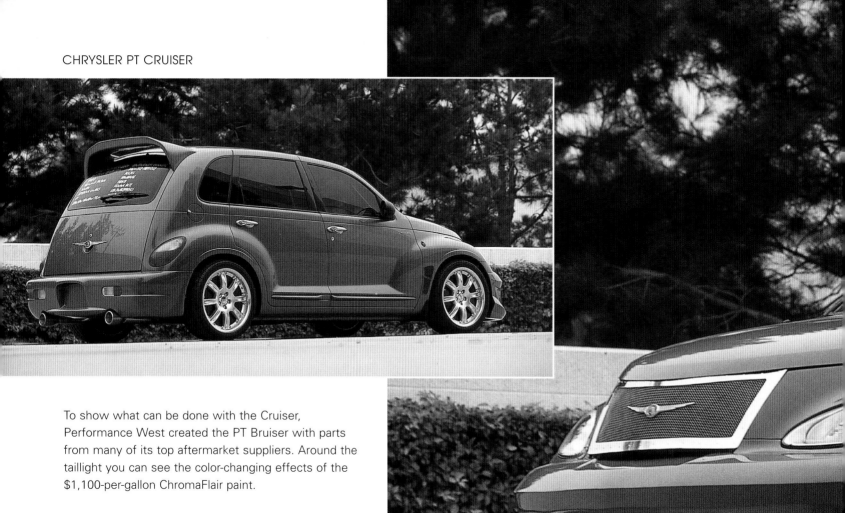

To show what can be done with the Cruiser, Performance West created the PT Bruiser with parts from many of its top aftermarket suppliers. Around the taillight you can see the color-changing effects of the $1,100-per-gallon ChromaFlair paint.

Lowered, with a new rear valance panel, dual exhaust tips, and a roof spoiler, the PT Bruiser has a nicely settled-down look. Race Truck Trends built the Bruiser using body panels made by Xenon.

Sparco did the Bruiser's interior using leather-upholstered carbon-fiber bucket seats, four-point harnesses, a full rollcage, and a carbon-fiber dash cover. The right-side airbag panel now has added gauges. On the center console is the trip handle for the on-board fire extinguisher system. *John Lamm*

large driving lights. At the rear, twin chromed tailpipes add a sporty flair. And the exterior badges have been streamlined to keep with the rodder look. Unlike a side-hinged door on a true sedan delivery, the Panel Cruiser retains the stock liftgate of the PT Cruiser.

Beneath the hood, the 2.4-liter dohc four is boosted, and like the GT Cruiser, the Panel Cruiser was outfitted with a turbocharger. That engine was rated at

200 horsepower but torque, in this instance, was listed at 200 ft-lb. The Panel Cruiser also sported the Neon ACR five-speed manual transaxle.

"This concept is a good example of how we're approaching new styles, while staying true to the heritage of the Chrysler brand," Tom Gale said. "We've developed a stylish and exciting vehicle to drive."

The PT Cruiser's stock grille is replaced with this mesh grille, adding a retro touch. All Bruiser pieces, from the body panels to the supercharged engine, can be bought and added separately . . . but the entire package doubles the Cruiser's $20,000 price tag. *John Lamm*

BBS supplied the Bruiser's 18-inch spoked modular alloy wheels, which wear Continental tires. Fitted inside the wheels are carbon fiber discs that add a nice high-tech background, while hiding the car's huge Brembo disc brakes. *John Lamm*

Despite the rave reviews for both the GT Cruiser and Panel Cruiser, it may be some time before either is produced. In the meantime, Chrysler is counting on the aftermarket to run with PT Cruiser customization. Already various aftermarket suppliers have been working on woody and custom-painted versions of the PT Cruiser.

As we have seen, the powertrain packaging was a major challenge for the designers of the PT Cruiser. Additional performance will certainly come from the aftermarket first, most likely in the form of turbo- or supercharging. And as Chrysler has demonstrated by building both versions, it's likely that a boosted version

of the PT Cruiser, perhaps as early as six months after launch, will come from the factory. And don't forget all-wheel drive. The PT Cruizer concept car that bowed alongside the production PT Cruiser at the 1999 Detroit show sported both a full-roof canvas soft top and all-wheel drive. While at the time, some company insiders said the all-wheel-drive version would come about a year after launch, they have since pushed that estimate back to some future, unspecified date. After all, if the company is building all it can sell, why add complexity and cost to a vehicle that promotes its low price as one of its virtues?

In fact, the success of the PT Cruiser out of the box will determine how long those who are anxious for variations on a theme will have to wait. But the beauty of this breakthrough concept is its flexibility, and already imaginations are running wild, especially on the Internet, where dozens of sites devoted to the PT Cruiser have sprung up, in addition to the Chrysler-sponsored site that has drawn more than a half-million visitors.

Beyond a panel wagon, there's talk of a convertible or two-door model similar to the three-door Pronto Cruiser concept, or even one with a trunk like a modern interpretation of the classic three-window coupe.

What is it about the PT Cruiser that has triggered this instant love affair? Certainly the overall size and versatility of the PT Cruiser fit the lifestyles of many different kinds of people.

A. C. "Bud" Liebler, senior vice president of marketing, said "Everyone sees this vehicle differently because they project their personal philosophy to define PT Cruiser on their own terms. The PT Cruiser can be whatever the individual owner wants it to be and fits any lifestyle."

Liebler added that attitudes and self-perception rather than demographics define prospective customers. As a result, PT Cruiser cuts across a broad swath of ages, incomes, and lifestyles. Buyers tend to be adventurous in their hobbies and travel, and enjoy being the first on the block with new technology.

While there have been vehicles in this class that have attempted to offer this kind of versatility, none have struck the same emotional chord. It all boils down to styling. The PT Cruiser has come along at a time when not only do boxy minivans all look alike, but small cars in general look anonymous. By combining the functionality of both an economy car and a minivan into something that looks totally different, yet familiar,

Quickly fixing complaints about the Cruiser's lack of power, Kenne-Bell gave the Bruiser's engine a belt-driven supercharger, an intercooler, and nitrous-oxide injection. Brake horsepower is 271, but it can shoot to 325 horsepower with the nitrous switched on . . . and it's all street legal. *John Lamm*

thanks to the retro cues, Chrysler has cut through a crowded marketplace with a vehicle that possesses a genuine, emotional allure.

"A PT Cruiser can be whatever the individual owner wants it to be," concludes Tom Gale. "It fits any lifestyle. Some may see it as a tribute to the classic era, some as a street rod, others as a multifaceted and functional light truck in a class of its own. There's really nothing like it on the road today."

APPENDIX A: SPECIFICATIONS

All dimensions are in inches (with millimeters in parenthesis) unless otherwise noted.

General Information

Body Style	Four-door multipurpose hatchback
Assembly Plant	Toluca, Mexico
Introduction Date	Spring 2000
EPA Vehicle Class	Two-wheel-drive special-purpose vehicle

Engine: 2.4-liter, dohc, 16-valve sequential multiport injected (SMPI)/I-4

Type and Description	Four-cylinder, inline, liquid-cooled
Displacement	148.2 ci (2,429 cc)
Bore x Stroke	3.44x3.98 (87.5x101)
Valve System	Belt-driven dohc, 16 valves, stamped-steel roller followers, hydraulic lash adjusters
Fuel Injection	Sequential multiport, electronic
Construction	Cast-iron block, cast-iron bedplate, aluminum alloy head, balance shafts
Compression Ratio	9.4:1
Power (SAE net)	150 bhp (112 kW) @ 5,500 rpm - 62.5 bhp/liter
Torque (SAE net)	162 ft-lb (220 N-m) @ 4,000 rpm
Max. Engine Speed	6,240 rpm electronically limited
Fuel Requirement	Unleaded regular, 87 octane R+M/2
Oil Capacity	4.5 qt (4.3 L) plus filter
Coolant Capacity	7.4 qt (7 L)
Emission Control	Three-way catalyst, heated oxygen sensor, EGR
Max. Gross Trailer Weight	1,000 lbs (450 kg) (20 sq ft maximum allowable frontal area)
EPA Fuel Economy (MPG City/Hwy)	20/26 manual; 20/25 automatic
Alternator	120 A
Battery	540 A, Group 26R, maintenance-free

Engines: 2.0-liter, dohc, 16-valve smpi I-4

Type and Description	Four-cylinder, inline, liquid-cooled
Displacement	121.8 ci (1,995 cc)
Bore x Stroke	3.44x3.27 in (87.5x83 mm)

Valve System . . . . Belt-driven dohc, 16 valves, stamped-steel roller
followers, hydraulic lash adjusters
Fuel Injection . . . . Sequential multiport, electronic, returnless
Construction . . . . Cast-iron block and bedplate, aluminum alloy head,
structural aluminum oil pan
Compression Ratio. 9.6:1
Power (SAE net). . . . . 140 bhp (104 kW) @ 5,700 rpm - 70 bhp/liter
Torque (SAE net). . . . . 139 ft-lb (188 N-m) @ 4,150 rpm
Max. Engine Speed . . . . 6,752 rpm manual trans., 6,720 automatic trans.,
electronically limited
Fuel Requirement . . . . Unleaded, 90 octane R+M/2
Oil Capacity. . . . . 4 qt (3.8 L) plus filter
Coolant Capacity . . . . 7.4 qt (7.0 L)
Emission Controls . . . . Three-way catalyst, twin heated oxygen sensors (a)
Max. Gross Trailer Weight . . . . 1,000 kg (450 kg) (2.98 sq m maximum allowable
frontal area)

Fuel Economy, European
(l/100 km urban/extra-urban) . . . . 11.5/7.0 manual, 13.1/7.9 automatic
Alternator . . . . 120 A
Battery . . . . 450 A, Group 26R, maintenance-free
(a) Meets Euro III requirements

Transaxle: Manual Five-Speed
Description. . . . . Five-speed, overdrive; synchronized in all forward
ratios; cable-operated, three-plane shifter

Gear Ratios
1st 3.50
2nd 1.96
3rd 1.36
4th 0.971
5th 0.811
Reverse (a) 3.42
Final Drive. 3.94
Overall Top Gear 3.20
(a) Includes reverse brake

119

Transaxles: Automatic, Four-Speed Overdrive

Description. . . . . Electronic control, electronically modulated
converter clutch

Gear Ratios
1st 2.84
2nd 1.57
3rd 1.00
4th 0.69
Reverse. 2.21
Effective Final Drive . . . . 3.91 w/2.4-liter engine, 4.07 w/2-liter engine
Overall Top Gear . . . . 2.694 w/2.4-liter engine, 2.808 w/2-liter engine

Dimensions and Capacities

Wheelbase 103.0 (2,616)
Track, Front. 58.3 (1,481)
Track, Rear. 58.2 (1,478)
Overall Length. 168.8 (4,288)
Overall Width @ Frt. Seat 67.1 (1,705)
Overall Height (a) 63.0 (1,601)
Ground Clearance (a) 6.5 (166)
Curb Weight, lbs (kg), estimated . . . . 3,123 (1,418) - 2.4-liter engine w/man. trans.
3,187 (1,446) - 2.4-liter engine w/auto. trans.
3,049 (1,383) - 2-liter engine w/man. trans.
3,133 (1,421) - 2-liter engine w/auto. trans.
Weight Distribution, % F/R . . . . 59/41 - 2.4-liter engine
w/manual transmission at curb weight
Drag Coefficient. 0.379
Fuel Tank Capacity . . . . 15 gal (57 L)
Payload (b). . . . . 865 lbs (392 kg)
(a) At curb weight
(b) Includes all driver, passengers, and cargo

Accommodations

Seating Capacity, F/R. 2/3
Front
    Head Room. 40.4 (1,026)
    Leg Room 40.6 (1,032)
    Shoulder Room. 54.6 (1,386)

Hip Room 54.0 (1,372)
SAE Volume . . . . 51.8 cft (1.47 cu m)
Seat Travel . . . . 9.0 (228) horizontal - All, 1.38 (35) vertical
                                w/optional power height adjuster
Recliner Range . . . . 54°

Rear

Head Room 39.6 (1,006)
Leg Room 40.8 (1,038)
Knee Clearance 2.6 (65.8)
Shoulder Room 53.9 (1,368.4)
Hip Room 46.8 (1,188)
SAE Volume . . . . 49.4 cft (1.40 cu m.)
SAE Cargo Volume Aft of Rear Seat . . . . 19.0 cft (0.538 cu m)
SAE Cargo Volume Rear Seats Out . . . . 64.2 cf. (1.82 cu m)
Load Capacity . . . . 115 lbs (52 kg)
EPA Interior Volume Index . . . . 120.2 c ft (3.41 cu m.)

Body

Layout . . . . Transverse front engine, front-wheel drive
Construction . . . . Steel Unibody

Suspension

Front . . . . MacPherson struts, asymmetrical lower control
                                arms, coil springs, and link-type stabilizer bar

Rear . . . . Trailing arms, twist beam axle w/integral tubular
                                stabilizer bar, Watts linkage, coil springs, gas-
                                charged shock absorbers, and linked stabilizer
                                bar

Steering

Type . . . . Power rack and pinion
Overall Ratio 18:1
Steering Turns (lock-to-lock) 3.0
Turning Diameter (curb-to-curb) . . . . 36.5 ft (11.1 m) w/base tires and manual
                                transmission; 39.7 ft (12.1 m) w/16-inch tires
                                and automatic transmission

Wheels
Standard
     Type and Material . . . . Steel disc
     Size 15x6
Optional
     Type and Material . . . . Cast aluminum
     Size 16x6

Tires
Size and Type . . . . P195/65R15 all-season touring (a)
     Mfr. and Model . . . . Goodyear Eagle LS
     Revs/Mile (Km) 835 (519)
Size and Type . . . . 195/65HR15 all-season performance (b)
     Mfr. and Model . . . . Goodyear NCT5
     Revs/Mile (Km) 832 (517)
Size and Type . . . . 205/55HR16 all-season performance (c)
     Mfr. and Model . . . . Goodyear NCT5
     Revs/Mile (Km) . . . . 837(520)
Size and Type . . . . P205/55R16 all season (d)
     Mfr. and Model . . . . Goodyear Eagle LS
     Revs/Mile (Km) 836 (519)
Size and Type . . . . 185/65HR15 all-season performance (e)
     Mfr. and Model . . . . Goodyear Eagle Vector
     Revs/Mile (Km) 854 (531)
(a) Std. except Europe and RHD
(b) Std. Europe and RHD
(c) Opt. Europe and RHD
(d) Opt. except Europe and RHD
(e) Opt. Europe and RHD

Brakes
Standard
Front
     Size and Type . . . . 10.94 x 0.9 (278 x 23) vented disc w/single-piston
                                       sliding caliper
     Swept Area . . . . 198.5 sq in (1,281 sq cm)
Rear
     Size and Type . . . . 8.66 x 1.57 (220 x 40) drum
     Swept Area . . . . 86 sq in (556 sq cm)

Power Assist Type. . . . . Tandem diaphragm, vacuum
Optional
Front
    Size and Type . . . . Same as standard w/ABS
Rear
    Size and Type . . . . 10.62 x 0.35 (269 x 9) solid disc w/single-piston
                                      sliding caliper and ABS
    Swept Area . . . . 173.4 sq in (1,119 sq cm)
    Power Assist Type. . . . . Same as standard

APPENDIX B: FEATURES

Legend:
S = Standard
O = Optional, alone or in a group
O* = No-charge option
P = Available only in a package

Exterior	Standard	Limited Edition
Appliqué, B-pillar, black	S	S
Badge, Limited Edition	—	S
Bracket, front license plate (standard in Canada)	O	O
Colors (Aquamarine Metallic, Black, Bright Silver Metallic, Deep Cranberry Pearl Coat, Inferno Red Tinted Pearl Coat, Patriot Blue Pearl Coat, Shale Green Metallic, Stone White, and Taupe Frost Metallic)	O*	O*
Defroster, rear window	S	S
Door Handles, bright	S	S
Fascias		
Front, accent/body color (includes 5-mph impact protection)	S	S
Rear, accent/body color (includes 5-mph impact protection)	S	S
Glass		
Solar control in all windows	S	S
Deep-tint in rear door, quarter, and liftgate windows, Solar control in windshield and front doors	P	S
Headlamps, Halogen, quad	S	S
Lamps		
Backup	S	S
Front Fog (includes instrument cluster warning indicator)	P	S

Park/Turn Daytime Running (Canada only)	S	S
Lock Bezels, door and liftgate, bright	S	S
Mirrors		
Manual, remote control	S	—
Power, remote control, heated, foldaway	P	S
Moonroof, power (tilt/vent/slide with solar glass, sliding sunshade, and one-touch-open feature) (optional in Canada)	P	S
Molding, bodyside (body color)	S	S
Roof Rack (includes two continuously adjustable cross bars w/side-by-side "spoiler appearance" stowage capability, and quick-release latches)	O	O
Windshield Wipers, two-speed w/variable intermittent delay and mist wipe	S	S
Wiper/Washer, rear window w/fixed intermittent delay	S	S
Interior		
Assist Handles (4)	P	S
Cargo Net	P	S
Carpet, passenger and cargo compartment	S	S
Climate Control		
Air Conditioning w/fluidic instrument panel outlets	S	S
Heater Outlets, floor, front, and rear	S	S
Coat Hooks (2), rear	S	S
Color (Dark Taupe/Light Pearl Beige)	S	S
Console		
Full-Length Floor (includes two front, one center, and one rear cup holders; removable coin holder; pencil tray; CD/cassette holder; front storage slot; center storage tray)	S	S
Overhead (includes driver and passenger map/reading lamps w/ integral on/off switches, compass, and outside temperature display w/US/metric switch and standard rearview mirror)	O	S
Door Trim Panels w/storage pockets, front and rear	S	S
Floor Mats		
Front and Rear	S	—
Front and Rear, fronts embroidered w/PT Cruiser logo	P	S
Glove Box, locking	S	S
Instrumentation		
Gauges (speedometer, tachometer, fuel level, and engine temperature)	S	S
Digital Display (odometer, trip odometer, door ajar, and liftgate ajar)	S	S
Warning Lamps (low fuel, seatbelts, brake system, check engine, high-beam headlamps, airbags, engine oil pressure, electrical system, and engine overheat)	S	S
Turn Signal Indicators (on instrument cluster bezel)	S	S

Instrument Cluster Bezel and Passenger Airbag Door (high-gloss color-keyed to Aquamarine, Deep Cranberry, Inferno Red, Patriot Blue, and Shale Green exterior colors with Black, Bright Silver, Stone White, and Taupe Frost accent colors)	S	S
Lamps		
Cargo Compartment (includes theater dimming and automatic time out)	S	S
Front Dome (includes theater dimming and automatic time out)	S	S
Mirrors		
Rearview Day/Night, manual	S	S
Day/Night, manual, w/reading lamps	P	—
Electrical Power Outlet, 12-volt, center console, ignition fed	S	S
Radios		
Antenna, fixed, fluted	S	S
AM/FM Stereo w/cassette player and CD changer controls	S	S
AM/FM Stereo w/cassette and CD players	O	O
Speakers, six, premium	S	S
Steering Column, tilt	S	S
Seat and Door Trim Bolster Material		
Tipton II cloth	S	—
Leather-Trimmed Seats w/preferred suede accents and vinyl door bolsters	—	S
Seats, Front		
Reclining Low-Back Bucket w/two-way adjustable, locking head restraints, driver inboard pivoting armrest, and passenger seatback storage net	S	—
Reclining Low-Back Bucket w/four-way adjustable, locking head restraints, driver inboard pivoting armrest, and driver and passenger seatback storage nets	—	S
Fold Flat, Front Passenger Seat (includes seatback tray)	P	S
Power Height Adjuster, driver	O	S
Seats, Rear		
Fold and Tumble w/65/35 split cushion and back, and quick-release removal system	S	S
Head Restraints, rear seat outboard, two-way adjustable, locking	P	S
Shift Knob, leather wrapped (w/automatic)	P	S
Speed Control (includes steering column controls and instrument cluster indicator lamp)	O	S
Steering Wheel		
Molded Urethane Rim	S	S
Leather Wrapped	P	S
Storage Drawer, underseat (late availability)	P	S
Sun Visors		
Sliding w/Covered Mirrors	S	—

Sliding w/Lighted Vanity Mirrors	P	S
Utility Panel, removable, five-position	S	S
Windows, power, front w/one-touch-open switches and rear	S	S

Powertrain and Chassis

2.4-liter 4-cylinder dohc 16V SMPI engine	S	S
5-Speed Manual w/ball shifter	S	S
4-Speed Automatic	O	O

Brakes

Power Front Disc/Rear Drum	S	S
Anti-Lock Four-Wheel Disc (includes traction control)	O	O
Engine Block Heater (standard in Canada)	O	O
Exhaust Tip, chrome	P	S
Steering, power rack and pinion	S	S
Stabilizer Bars, front and rear	S	S

Suspension

Normal Duty (includes MacPherson strut independent front suspension and twist beam rear suspension w/coil springs and Watts linkage)	S	S
Touring Tuned	P	S
Tire, Spare, compact w/alloy wheel	S	S

Tires

P195/65R15 Black Sidewall All-Season Touring	S	S
P205/55R16 Black Sidewall All-Season Touring	P	S
Wheel Covers, 15-inch, bolt-on type w/bright retaining nuts	S	—

Wheels

15x6.0-inch Steel	S	—
16x6.0-inch Alloy, painted (credit option on Limited Edition)	P	O
16x6.0-inch Alloy, chrome plated	P	S

Safety and Security

Accident Response Illumination System	S	S
Keyless Entry, remote (includes two transmitters and panic alarm)	P	S

Locks

Power (includes central locking and customer programmable automatic locking)	P	S
Rear Door Child Protection	S	S

Restraint Systems

Airbags, front, Next Generation	S	S
Airbags, supplemental side, front outboard occupant (includes seatback storage nets and carpet inserts) (not available in Mexico)	O	S
Seatbelts, three-point, w/pre-tensioners, constant-force retractors,		

traveling inboard buckles, and adjustable turning loops, front; three-point, all rear positions	S	S
Security Alarm (includes horn pulse, flashing headlamps and park lamps, and instrument cluster warning lamp) (standard in Mexico)	P	S
Sentry Key Theft Deterrent System (standard in Mexico)	P	S
User-Ready LATCH Child Seat Anchorage System (lower anchors and tether-ready upper anchors)	S	S
Warning Chimes (key in ignition, headlamps on, low fuel, or front seatbelt not buckled)	S	S

Equipment Packages/Groups

2DF Equipment Package

Light Group (see below); fold-flat front passenger seat; two-way adjustable, locking rear seat outboard head restraints; cargo net; interior assist handles (4); front passenger underseat storage drawer; sunscreen glass; power, heated, foldaway mirrors; remote keyless entry w/2 transmitters; Sentry Key theft deterrent system, power locks w/central locking and customer programmable rolling locks and security alarm system	O	—

Light Group

Sliding sun visors w/illuminated vanity mirrors, rearview mirror w/reading lamps (std. mirror used w/overhead console), auxiliary 12-volt electrical power outlets front (center stack, battery fed) and rear (cargo area, ignition fed), and console flood lamp	O	S

Luxury Touring Group

Front floor mats w/embroidered PT Cruiser logo, leather-wrapped shift knob w/automatic transaxle, fog lamps, chrome exhaust tip, leather-wrapped steering wheel, touring-tuned suspension, P205/55R16 black sidewall all-season touring tires, 16-inch chrome-plated alloy wheels and Touring Edition badge (badge deleted on Limited Edition)	O	S

Moonroof Group

Power moonroof w/one-touch-open switch and sliding sunshade, Light Group, interior assist handles (4) overhead console w/compass and temperature display	O	S

Touring Group

Fog lamps, Touring Edition badge, touring-tuned suspension, P205/55R16 black sidewall all-season touring tires and 16-inch painted aluminum wheels (NA w/Luxury Touring Group)	O	—

Note: Feature availability varies among equipment packages. The information shown is preliminary and based on data available at the time of publication.

INDEX